THE
OFF-LOOM
WEAVING
BOOK

THE OFF-LOOM WEAVING BOOK

Rose Naumann
and
Raymond Hull

CHARLES SCRIBNER'S SONS, NEW YORK

All figures by Helmut Hirnschall.

All photographs by Mark Kaarremaa and Ulli Steltzer
(except where otherwise indicated).

1 3 5 7 9 11 13 15 17 19 MD/C 20 18 16 14 12 10 8 6 4 2

Printed in the United States of America
Library of Congress Catalog Card Number 72-11139
SBN 684-13303-2 (cloth)

CONTENTS

Varieties in texture: tapestry, loops, Ghiordes knots.

CHAPTER 1

~~~~~~~~~~~~~~~~~~~~~~~~~~~~~~~~

SPEAKING OF WEAVING

In this book I am going to tell you of the joys and rewards of weaving without a loom; I will show you how to escape from the rush and noise of everyday life and return to the quiet, leisurely pace of earlier times. The simple methods I am going to describe will, almost like magic, enable you to create beautiful, useful things for yourself, your family, and your friends: neckties, belts, purses, shawls, cushion covers, blankets, ponchos, vests, wall hangings, and many more.

This is an economical hobby; with a minimum of materials, you can achieve maximum results. I have seen weavers make a number of articles without any expense at all, by using materials lying around their homes. Or, to start completely from scratch, you need spend less than five dollars.

Are you conservation-minded? Then you'll enjoy recycling scrap and salvaged materials: cloth and wool reclaimed from old garments or left over from dressmaking and knitting, string of many kinds, sheet plastic, fur, feathers, and so on. All these things that might have been wasted can be saved for your weaving projects.

You can do off-loom weaving wherever you live, whether you have a big house with a workroom specially for your hobbies, or whether you live in a small apartment. The apparatus and materials for off-loom weaving are compact; they can be stored in a single drawer, or one shelf of a closet. Off-loom weaving makes no noise and no mess.

Weaving has special advantages for busy people. Some arts and crafts require fairly large segments of time. Some are messy; with pottery, for instance, you put on old clothes, get yourself slathered with wet clay up to the elbows, and then have to scrub yourself clean afterward.

Not so with weaving! Pick up your project at any time and work on it for five minutes or two hours. Put it down when you like; it will be ready for you whenever you want to resume work; and you, with hands and clothes spotless, can turn at once to something else.

Do you—like most of us—sometimes feel tense and nervous? Then you'll find a potent therapy in weaving. The light, rhythmical motion of arms, hands and fingers, and the enforced, yet pleasurable, concentration help soothe your mind; and, when things have gone wrong at home or at work, it's a positive delight to see your weaving turn out right, to feel it growing under your hands. Life in general can't always be as we want it; weaving can be so. To be sure, you'll make some mistakes, but mistakes in weaving can be corrected; and with a little care and patience, you can be sure of success.

Yet for most people the greatest satisfaction of weaving is that it offers such a good outlet for their creativity. A lot of men and women, unfortunately, find that their work and their home life become a routine, a repetition of dull tasks controlled by the clock and by the demands of other people.

But in off-loom weaving you'll discover unlimited scope for originality in choosing materials, in creating your own designs, in discovering new techniques and inventing new bits of equipment.

Every student I've taught, every weaver I've known, has enjoyed such experiences; you will enjoy them. too. Once you have completed a few fairly straightforward projects, and mastered the basic techniques, you can go on to taste the thrills of creative weaving.

WHAT IS WEAVING?

Weaving is the systematic interlacing of two or more sets of elements usually, but not necessarily, at right angles, to form a coherent structure, that is, a structure that holds itself together. Chapter 2 describes, and gives some suggestions for obtaining and preparing, the many kinds of materials that may be used.

The finished piece of weaving may be thin, like a wall hanging; it may be thick, like a rug; it may be more or less rigid, like a bamboo placemat; it may be three-dimensional, like a basket.

Weaving is one of the oldest handicrafts. Plaiting, braiding, knotting and netting, for making hammocks, carrying bags, hairnets and fishnets, have been practiced for at least four thousand years in many parts of the world.

Card weaving (or "tablet weaving"), a method of producing narrow strips of fabric in complex patterns, is equally ancient; it was practiced in Egypt, Europe, and China.

Basket weaving, with reeds and grasses, antedated the invention of the potter's wheel; early potters would line a basket with clay to produce a pot.

Weaving methods, naturally, varied from place to place, according to the climate and to the materials available. In hot countries, thin fabrics were woven from silk, cotton, and linen. In cold regions, wool and goat hair were woven into thick fabrics, some of them long-piled for extra warmth, in imitation of animal pelts. (Piled rugs, of course, were originally a man-made substitute for fur rugs, used as insulation on cold floors.)

The weavers of Europe, from medieval times, were influenced by Chinese and Mideastern techniques. Belgium and France, in particular, developed tapestry weaving to a very high artistic level.

When white men came to central America in the sixteenth century, they found efficient weaving techniques many centuries old. With backstrap looms, wool from the llama, alpaca and vi-

Navajos spinning and weaving. (*Photo: Ulli Steltzer*)

cuna, and a rich palette of dyestuffs, the Peruvians made tapestries and clothes in elaborate patterns and many colors. Later explorers found the Indians of the Pacific Northwest weaving beautiful blankets of goat hair, dog hair, and spun cedar bark on weighted warps. The Maoris of New Zealand used a twining technique to weave skirts, raincapes, and bed covers.

Weaving, all over the world, was for thousands of years a home craft: using mainly the simple methods described in this book, families produced cloth for their own garments and bedding or wove, in fairly small quantities, fabrics for sale or barter. But the industrial revolution put an end to cottage industries; spinning and weaving began to be done by machines in large factories.

Factory weaving has not ceased, and is not likely to; yet, in recent years there has been a vigorous revival of interest in weaving at home, as an enjoyable craft, as an art and—for some people—as a profitable part-time or full-time business. The personal satisfaction that the old-time weaver knew is attainable today for anyone who will apply a moderate amount of dexterity and patience to the projects described in this book.

SOME TECHNICAL TERMS

Warp

For weaving a typical piece of cloth, the warp is the first set of threads to be put in place—the base upon which the weaving is done. The warp threads usually are parallel, and lie along the longer dimension of the work. To make a cloth belt 42 inches by 7 inches, you would set up your warp threads somewhat more than 42 inches long (to allow for wastage at the ends).

According to the weaving technique you use, the warp may show prominently in the finished work; it may show only slightly; or it may be quite concealed. This point, naturally, will influence your selection of the material to be used as warp.

One important point: warp must be strong. When first set up on the frame or other support, it is strained fairly tight. As you weave, you raise, lower, and otherwise manipulate each warp thread many times; you will notice the warp gradually becoming tighter than it was at the start. It must withstand this handling and tension without breaking, and without excessive stretching.

So, by using a fairly strong warp, you find that your finished work is strong and holds its shape.

Weft

The weft is the element that is interlaced with the warp, passing over and under it in some systematic way. This over-and-under arrangement has two functions. It holds the finished cloth or other structure firmly together. It largely determines the ap-

Simple weaving frame made of tree branches. (*Photo: Ulli Stelzer*)

pearance and texture of the finished product. Suppose you weave two pieces of cloth from identical warp and weft fibers; in one you use an over-one-and-under-one interlacing (a "tabby" weave) and in the other an over-two-and-under-two interlacing, with two wefts at once (a "basket" weave); the two pieces of cloth will look noticeably different.

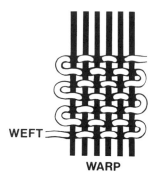

Warp and weft on tabby weave.   Basket weave.

There is no need to use the same weft all through a piece of work; you can use assorted thicknesses, textures, and colors, or even entirely different materials—for example, string, raffia, or feathers in a piece of weaving mainly made of wool. These different wefts, introduced in a pattern or at random, can produce a pleasing variety in your work.

The weft receives less manipulation and undergoes less strain than the warp; so it can be, if you wish, more delicate or more stretchable than the warp.

A single thread of weft, when laid across the warp, is called a "shot" (some weavers call it a "pick").

Web

The web is the material formed by weaving. The word "web" comes from the Anglo-Saxon root *wefan* that also supplied the word "weft." (A spider's web is a piece of weaving, although its threads are held together by adhesive instead of by under-and-over placement.)

Shed

In darning, the needle is slid over one warp thread and under the next to produce the desired web.

For weaving on a bigger scale, you will often find it convenient to raise a number of warp threads simultaneously, leaving the others in their original position; this makes a space between the upper and lower warps. This space is called a shed. Through this shed the weft can be quickly passed.

Beating In

To leave the weft just where you inserted it would produce an uneven web. For most kinds of weaving you will need to move the newly inserted shot so that it lies parallel to the rest of the weft. This process is called "beating in." On narrow webs (e.g., belts,

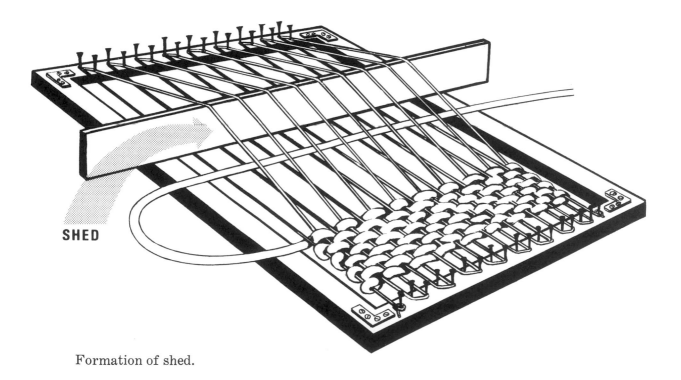

SHED

Formation of shed.

Beating in with a fork.

ties) you can do it with your fingers; on wider webs it is easier to use a coarse-toothed comb or a dinner fork.

Careful beating in, by ensuring that the wefts are evenly spaced, gives a uniform web. For certain techniques, by beating in vigorously you press the wefts tightly together; gentle beating in leaves the wefts farther apart.

Loom

A loom performs the three stages of the weaving process: making the shed, passing the weft, and beating in. On industrial power-looms, all the work is done mechanically; the operator merely watches to see that everything is working properly.

Most home looms use hand-levers or pedals to make the shed; the warp, wound on a shuttle, is passed back and forth, and the beating in is done by hand.

Such a hand-loom is by no means easy to use. Putting in the warp is a slow job for two people, and very laborious for one.

Many home looms are bulky, taking up nearly as much space as a baby grand piano. They are far from cheap; prices run up into the hundreds of dollars.

WHY OFF-LOOM WEAVING?

Please don't think that I am trying to denounce loom weaving. I have a big loom myself, and use it often. Yet, before you go to the expense of buying a loom and the labor of learning to use it, I would strongly advise you to master the off-loom weaving skills described here. In this way you can discover whether you really do enjoy weaving; you can develop the qualities—dexterity, creativity, color sense—that tend toward success in weaving. You can do this at a trifling expenditure of time and money, and you can have a lot of pleasure in the process.

CHAPTER 2

~~~~~~

MATERIALS FOR OFF-LOOM WEAVING

The typical loom, by its construction and operating techniques, restricts a weaver to the use of flexible materials; off-loom weaving permits you a much wider choice. Indeed, the possibilities are almost unlimited. You can walk through city, park or garden, along the beach, into the woods; you can explore a hardware store or a shipyard; you will see the world with new eyes, continually discovering exciting new uses for familiar materials.

Before discussing sources of supply, costs, and methods of preparing materials for use, let us define some terms that apply to many of these materials.

STAPLE

All the natural weaving yarns (except silk), and some of the man-made ones, are composed of relatively short fibers twisted together. The staple length is the average length of the constituent fibers.

15

In cotton, for example, the staple length is about 1 inch. Wools of various qualities have staple lengths of 2½ to 5 inches. Mohair, from the Angora goat, runs from 9 to 12 inches. Alpaca has a staple length of 8 to 16 inches, with some special varieties going up to 36 inches. Jute—the fiber of a tall tropical plant—has a staple of 4 to 7 feet.

The synthetic fibers—rayon, nylon, etc.—can be made of any length desired (long monofilament fishlines, for example), but can also be produced in short or medium staple and spun into yarn in much the same way as cotton or wool.

SPINNING

Spinning is the process by which fibers are twisted into yarn. The fibers are all more or less rough so, when twisted together, they adhere, and form a long, continuous thread.

If yarn has only a few twists per inch, it is said to be *soft-twisted;* if it has many twists per inch, it is *hard-twisted.* A soft-twisted yarn tends to be actually softer than a hard-twisted; it yields more easily to lateral pressure, it stretches more, and will not stand so much wear and tear. A soft-twisted yarn, then, is not usually suitable for the warp; it would not stand the continual tension and the fairly vigorous manipulation involved in the weaving process. Hard-twisted yarns are generally better for warps; soft-twisted yarns have their place in the weft.

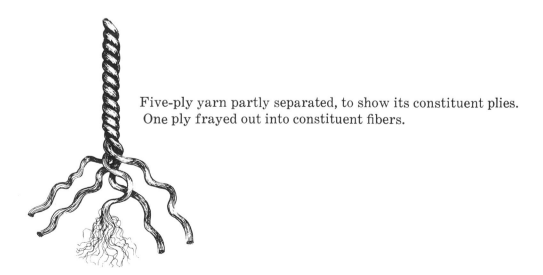

Five-ply yarn partly separated, to show its constituent plies. One ply frayed out into constituent fibers.

One thread, as it comes from the spinning wheel or machine, is called a single *ply*. Single-ply yarns are used for some purposes but, to make thicker, stronger yarns, several plies may be twisted together. When the yarns are plied together, they are twisted in the direction opposite to their first twist, which keeps the strands interlocked.

YARN NUMBERS

Most weavers buy yarn either by looking around the store and picking what they like or by mail, selecting from a manufacturer's sample card bearing pieces of the various colors, textures, and thicknesses.

Nevertheless, many writers about weaving, and some manufacturers, use a system of code numbers to indicate the thickness and structure of yarn. So here is a brief outline of the system.

For cotton, linen, wool, and worsted (worsted is made of wool, but more tightly twisted than ordinary wool yarn), No. 1 is the thickest single-ply yarn made. No. 2 is thinner than No. 1. No. 3 is thinner still, and so on; the larger the number, the thinner the yarn.

Yarns made of several plies twisted together have a double number.

United States System

The first number indicates the thickness of the individual plies; the second shows how many are twisted together, for example, 10/3 means 3 No. 10 plies; 15/5 means 5 No. 15 plies, and so on.

Canadian and British System

First comes the number of plies; the second number shows the thickness of each ply, for example, 2/9 means 2 No. 9 plies; 3/6 means 3 No. 6 plies.

So, when you read a weaving magazine, a dealer's price list, or the label on a yarn package, note where it comes from; then you can tell what the yarn numbers mean.

QUALITIES OF VARIOUS YARNS

Let's look at the more commonly used fibers, and see their advantages and disadvantages, as a guide to selecting materials for various kinds of work.

Wool

Wool is probably used by hand weavers more than any other fiber. It is very elastic; it will stretch, without breaking, up to 30 percent of its length, and snap back again. It is highly resilient; it can be bent 20,000 times without breaking and, after being crushed or crumpled, it springs back to its original shape. Various wools have tensile strengths ranging from 17,000 to 29,000 pounds per square inch; so in weaving, wool holds its tension if used as warp, and you can easily carry out the most complex manipulations with it as weft.

Wool has good insulating qualities, so makes warm garments, rugs, etc. It is fire-resistant, burning only while held in a direct flame. Raw wool (i.e., still retaining its natural oils) repels water, and can be made into rainproof hats, jackets, and sweaters.

Wool does have some disadvantages. Moths like to eat it. If exposed too long to direct sunlight it loses strength and becomes harsh in texture. It gets mildewed if kept in a damp, unventilated place. Processed wool (with natural oils removed) absorbs water readily, and shrinks when it gets wet; if wetted and compressed, it may become felted.

Wool can be obtained in a wide range of colors. It can be spun into just about any thickness you want—from the diameter of thick sewing-cotton up to the thickness of your little finger; and in many textures—smooth, rough, nubby, fluffy, straight, spiraled, looped, and so on. Manufacturers keep producing new varieties, and the best way to know what's available at any time is to look in a store or at a wholesaler's catalogue.

Many kinds of wool yarn can be bought fairly cheaply; but handcraft-supply stores sell handspun wool at high prices (up to

$16.00 a pound for some varieties). Also, you can sometimes get natural-colored wools—that is, undyed wool, retaining the original fleece color—in grays, browns and black, at premium prices.

The costly varieties are generally used only in fairly small amounts, to give special touches of texture or color to a project mainly of cheaper yarn.

For purposes where a specially hard-wearing yarn is desired, you can buy wool reinforced with a proportion of some tough synthetic fiber such as nylon.

Some Norwegian and Swedish rug-wools contain a proportion of cow hair to give them extra body; so, after the pile has been trodden on, it springs up again.

(*Note*: For anyone who wants to try producing yarn at home, wool is about the easiest fiber for spinning and dyeing.)

Cotton

Cotton, like wool, accepts dyeing easily and is available in a wide range of thicknesses. It is flexible and easy to work with, but is less elastic than wool; consequently it is useful for any purpose where stretching would be undesirable—in rug warps, for example.

Cotton shrinks much less than wool, but it creases and wrinkles very easily. It withstands laundering well, so is suitable for placemats, baby bibs, and other household items that need to be washed frequently.

Jute

The natural color of jute is brown, but it is now available in a number of rich colors (no delicate pastel shades, though), and a good range of thicknesses going all the way through fine and thick cord, up to medium or thick rope.

Spun jute is very strong; it makes a good, firm warp for the weaving frame and, with jute warp, you will find it easy to keep the edges of the web straight. However, jute has, so far as weaving is concerned, no elasticity at all; so, with a jute warp, you should use a wide tension stick, or use an adjustable frame, to allow for the inevitable take-up as weaving progresses.

Jute is specially suitable for techniques that involve knotting, because it keeps its diameter and shape even when tightly knotted. (Wool, because of its softness, is almost useless for such work.) Jute is excellent for net bags, wall hangings, macramé, rug warps, and such things.

Jute is cheap, about the cheapest of all weaving materials, in fact. It has been rather neglected by weavers in the past, but now that it is so easily available, it deserves much greater attention.

Silk

Silk, obtained from the cocoon of the silk-moth, is well known for its luster, smooth texture, and fineness of fiber. It is strong, elastic, and available in a good range of colors. Yet, because of its high price, most weavers would use silk only as weft, and in small quantities, to provide special accents of texture amid areas of other, cheaper yarns.

Linen

Linen, made from the fiber of the flax plant, is smooth, lustrous, and takes dyes well. It is stronger than cotton, but is rather expensive, and so is used for high-quality tapestry warps and similar special purposes.

Other Animal Fibers

The fibers mentioned in this section are not widely used by home weavers, but are sometimes available at fairly high prices.

Camel hair: usually sold undyed, in its natural sandy-brown color.

Alpaca: usually undyed; available in black, white, and several shades of brown.

Mohair: smoother and more lustrous than wool; takes dyes well, and is available in many colors.

Cashmere: available in natural colors of white, gray, and brown, also dyed.

Goat hair: available in white, black, and a variety of browns and grays; usually a loose-textured yarn, suitable only for use as weft.

Horse hair: a fairly thick yarn, usually available in dark brown.

Synthetic Fibers

The synthetic fibers are sold under a large number of trade-names; some of these names are merely different labels for the same thing; some differ widely in strength, elasticity, texture, and ease of dyeing. Many of the synthetics are made to look and feel very much like wool, cotton, or other natural fibers.

New synthetics and new trade-names appear so often that a book like this cannot keep up with them. By careful inspection of yarns in the store—look for color and luster; feel for elasticity, strength, and firmness—you can tell what would be suitable for any project you have in mind.

Metal Fibers

Gold, silver, and copper are available as thin wires or yarns in their natural colors; anodized aluminum comes in a range of brilliant colors.

String and Rope

String has long been used for knotting and netting, and as reinforcement for card-woven bands. The more attractive-looking forms of string and rope are now being much used in many forms of weaving: wall hangings, rugs, three-dimensional hangings, etc.

You can get string and rope of many thicknesses in cotton, hemp, jute, sisal, flax, rayon, and nylon.

Natural sisal is a pale straw-color; it may be dyed to any shade of light brown in coffee or tea. Oiled sisal is an attractive yellowish color. Sisal is extremely strong and quite stiff in texture; therefore it is specially suitable for three-dimensional works, as it holds a sculptured form better than other yarns. (Indeed, when properly handled, it can be made into a free-standing, woven sculpture!)

Binder twine—available inexpensively in very big balls—is a useful material, usually with a good orange-yellow color.

Manila rope is light brown. Tarred jute is dark brown, but quite stiff; tarred flax, also brown, is more flexible. (Interesting assortments of tarred strings, cords, and ropes can be seen at a ship chandler.)

I mentioned the dyeing of sisal; many other kinds of string and rope can also be dyed at home, to whatever colors you wish to use.

Braided strings and cords of various materials and thicknesses —mason line, sash cord, etc.—have interesting textures.

Different fibers show important differences in surface appearance: jute, for example, is dull; sisal is shiny.

Study and experiment with rope and string; you'll find they add much to your weaving.

Chenille

Chenille in cotton and rayon is often available in various colors, or you can buy it in white and dye it to suit your requirements.

Raffia

Raffia is good for weaving baskets. It is available in the natural color and an assortment of dyed colors.

An artificial raffia, made of rayon, is also available.

Unconventional Materials

You need not restrict yourself to the yarns that are made and sold specifically for weaving. There's a wide range of materials made for other purposes, or found in nature, that you can effectively use. Here are some suggestions.

Suede can be cut into strips of various widths and woven into many kinds of articles: wall hangings, cushion covers, handbags, etc. Suede comes in a wide range of colors, thicknesses, and textures. You can often get suede for nothing, by salvaging old articles that would otherwise have been discarded.

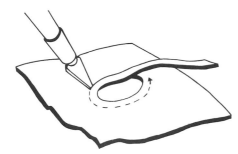

Spiral-cutting suede strip.

To get the longest possible strips from a piece of suede, cut around in spirals with a very sharp knife.

Nature products such as long pine needles, grasses, lichens, seashells, rushes, palm leaves, seedpods, twigs, long leaves and fronds from garden plants can be used. (Green leaves should first be dried.) You can get bamboo strips, or thin canes, by cutting up placemats, windowshades, or floormats made of the materials you want; these articles are usually quite cheap, even if you buy them new.

Feathers of many kinds, in their natural colors or dyed, can be woven into various objects for their great textural interest. You can get good ones from a feather duster.

Fur can often be obtained inexpensively—for example, by getting an outmoded fur coat at a junk-store and cutting it into strips. These can be woven very quickly into handbags, cushion covers, and such things.

Cloth, either new fabric or salvaged articles such as old bedsheets, can be dyed, cut into strips, and used for weft in making such things as rugs.

There is nowadays a growing interest in the salvaging and reusing of materials that would once have been destroyed as waste. Weavers can get extra satisfaction by thus turning old, useless materials into new, useful, beautiful artifacts. Go to it!

ESTIMATING QUANTITIES

A little simple arithmetic will give you a close estimate of how much yarn you need for any project.

Warp

First, find the number of warp threads: multiply the width of the web, in inches, by the number of warp threads per inch. To this number add any extra threads used for special purposes, for example double warp threads at selvedges.

Multiply the number of warp threads by the length of the warp, to get the total length of yarn in inches; divide by 36 to get length in yards.

Finally add 10 percent for wastage at the ends of the frame, etc.

For example, the sampler described in Chapter 4:

Width of web = 7 inches
Number of warp threads per inch = 4
Extra warp threads for selvedges = 2
Total number of warp threads: 7 x 4 + 2 = 30
Length of warp = 28 inches
Total length of warp yarn: $\frac{30 \times 28}{36}$ yards = 23⅓ yards
10 percent wastage allowance = 2⅓ yards
Total yarn required for warp = 25⅔ yards

Weft

To find the length of yarn for one shot of weft, take the proposed width of the web and add 25 percent. (This allows for wastage in beginning and ending lengths of yarn; it also allows

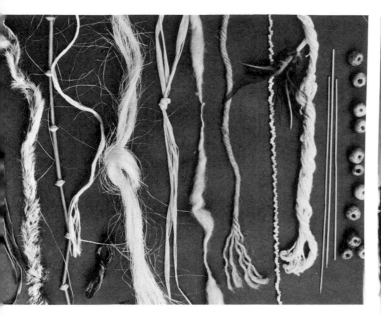

Weaving materials. *Left to right,* suede strip; fur strip; bamboo beads; synthetic fiber; copper wire; raw sisal; raffia; handspun wool; 5-ply jute; tiny shells; feathers; handspun silk; bamboo strips; clay beads.

Weaving materials at Handcraft House. *Center foreground,* raw sisal. *Left,* jute cord. *On wall,* cane for basketry.

for the fact that weft does not lie in a straight line, but in a series of curves, as it goes under and over the warp threads.)

For example, suppose you have a warp 10 inches wide; then the length of weft per shot should be 10 + 25 percent = 12½ inches.

The number of shots per inch depends on the thickness of yarn you use, and on how firmly you beat in. Thick yarn, lightly beaten in, might give 6 shots per inch; a thinner yarn, well beaten in, might require 12 shots to the inch.

To find this figure of shots per inch:

a) Weave a small sample section with the yarn you plan to use; or

b) Count the number of shots per inch on another piece of work using similar yarn and the same weave. (This is one use of a well-made sampler containing different yarns and different weaves.)

Materials from nature. *Left to right*, lichens on branch; iris seedpods; black lichen; gray lichen; tree fungus; honesty seeds; tree fungus.

Suppose you find your chosen yarn gives 10 shots per inch, and that the web is going to be 20 inches long. Then the yarn requirement will be:

$$\frac{12\frac{1}{2} \times 10 \times 20 \text{ yards}}{36} = 70 \text{ yards (approximately)}$$

Length and Weight

These estimates give you the length of yarn needed; but yarn is usually packaged and sold by weight. However, many manufacturers print on each package the length of yarn it contains. Often, too, the length-per-ounce figures for various yarns are shown on manufacturers' sample cards; or you can ask the retailer.

BUYING YARN

When you buy yarn for any project, it's wise to get *all* you need at once. If you don't get enough, you may go back to the store six weeks later and find that you can't exactly match the yarn that's already woven into your partly finished wall hanging.

That particular texture, thickness, or color may have been discontinued. Even if you find the same product from the same manufacturer, it may not be a perfect color-match. Various technical problems in dyeing make it difficult to obtain exactly the same color from batch after batch, even though identical chemicals were used.

So be warned: get *all* you need of any one kind of yarn, from *one* batch, at *one* time.

THE BUTTERFLY

A convenient way to handle weft yarn in weaving is to make it into a small skein called a butterfly.

1. Grasp the end of the yarn between first and second fingers, with 3 inches hanging down the back of the hand.

2. Wind between thumb and first finger, around the thumb, across the palm and between the third and fourth fingers.

3. Go around the fourth finger, back across the palm, and

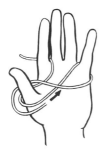

Beginning the butterfly.

around the thumb; you have now formed a figure 8.

4. Keep winding figure 8's until the butterfly is big enough to handle comfortably. Cut off the yarn and, with the end, tie two half-hitches around the center of the butterfly.

5. Take the butterfly off your fingers. To use it, pull on the unknotted end; the yarn will unravel smoothly from the center,

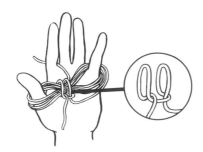

Completed butterfly.

without twisting or tangling, and the butterfly is compact enough to be manipulated in and out of the warps.

MEASURING YARN

For some purposes—card weaving, the weighted warp, etc.— you need to cut a number of pieces of yarn to a specified length. The quickest way is to use some kind of gauge; wind the yarn uniformly around this gauge and, with one cut, produce many pieces of identical length.

You can wind the yarn around the back of two chairs, placed the correct distance apart.

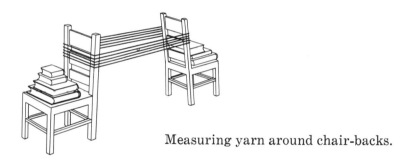

Measuring yarn around chair-backs.

Another convenient device is two C-clamps spaced the correct distance apart on a table.

Another simple method is to drive two pegs the correct distance apart in your lawn.

To set up one of these devices, cut one piece of yarn to the desired length; adjust the chair-backs, clamps, or pegs so that the sample piece exactly fits; wind on the number of turns of yarn you need, and cut.

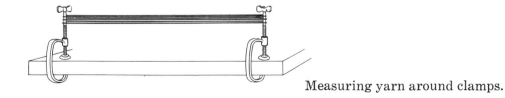

Measuring yarn around clamps.

CHAPTER 3

~~~~~~~~~~~~~~~~~~~~~~~~~~~~~~~~~~~~~~

WEAVING FRAMES

On a simple rectangular wooden frame, you can weave scores of different articles. This chapter describes several kinds of frames, and some small items of equipment that are used with them.

HOME-MADE FRAMES

Fixed Frame

Get some pieces of 1 x 2 inch wood (actual size when planed is about $\frac{3}{4}$ x $1\frac{1}{2}$ inches) and make a frame 20 x 28 inches, inside dimensions. The 20-inch lengths we will call the top and bottom, the 28-inch lengths, the sides.

There are three ways to join the corners.

You need some device at the top and bottom of the frame to hold the warp at the correct spacing and tension. So get some

Joining corners of weaving frame: miter joint and corrugated fasteners; angle irons; overlap and screws or nails.

1-inch finishing nails; ordinary nails with big heads would create difficulties when you want to remove the finished work.

For the first projects, you will use 4 warp threads per inch. But to drive nails in one line would tend to split the wood; it would also make it hard to manipulate the warp around the nails. So stagger them in two lines.

There is no need to drive the nails all the way across; leave about 4 inches clear space on each side of the frame, and make a double line of nails 12 inches long.

Drive the nails about halfway into the wood, not vertically, but sloping out toward the end of the frame. This prevents the warp from riding up on the nails as you weave.

The weaving frame: arrangement of nails; side view of nails.

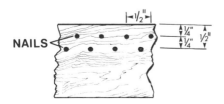

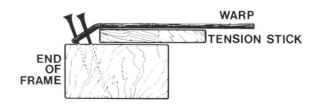

Adjustable Frames

It wastes warp yarn to make a small article on a big frame; it's annoying to find that your frame is an inch too short for the cushion cover or wall hanging you want to make. The remedy is to use an adjustable frame. Here are two designs.

Type 1: For rigidity, the top and bottom are fixed to the sides with nails and glue, or with screws. The sides have holes drilled at 2½-inch intervals. The movable crossbar is secured to the sides by bolts and butterfly nuts. Drive nails into the top and the crossbar to hold the warp.

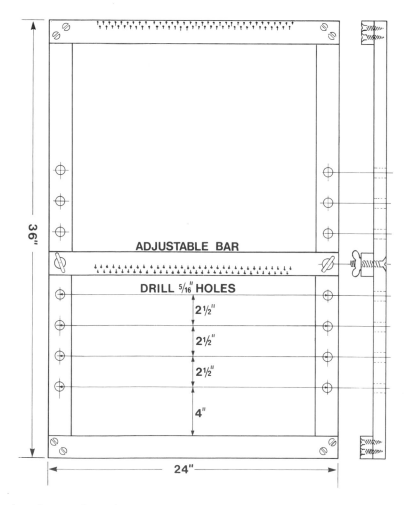

Adjustable weaving frame, type 1.

Type 2: The warp is not fastened to the top of the frame, but passes over a wooden slat or dowel that is tied by strong cords to the top. This allows easy adjustment for any desired length of web.

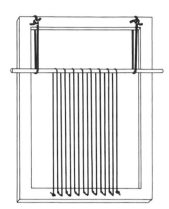

Adjustable weaving frame, type 2.

READY-MADE FRAMES

You can buy a canvas-stretcher at an artists' supply store. They come in a wide range of sizes, ready to assemble. To make the stretcher more rigid, some weavers add angle-irons at the corners.

An old picture-frame of the right size will serve the same purpose.

Hobby and craft supply stores sell commercially made weaving frames. Some of these are very small—about 10 x 10 inches—and would not be of much practical value. Others come in a range of larger sizes, up to about 30 x 30 inches.

TENSION STICK AND SHED STICK

Get two sticks 24 x 1½ x ¼ inches. The tension stick is laid flat on the frame, its edge right against the nails at the top, its ends projecting over the sides. The warp is going to be applied *over* this stick. (See diagram on page 30.) As the weaving progresses, the warp tightens up. When it becomes so tight that you cannot easily make a shed, remove the tension stick; this gives you a bit of slack and lets you complete the web.

If your frame is built with ends and sides overlapped, the tension stick may tend to fall down; if so, tie it in place with string or adhesive tape.

When the frame is warped, you insert the shed stick at right angles to the warp, under one thread, over the next, and so on, right across. Let it rest, until you are ready to weave, flat side down, a few inches projecting beyond each side of the frame.

Most weavers prefer to work with the frame on a slant; so to avoid having the shed stick slip down to the bottom, tie it to the top of the frame with a string at each end. (To keep the strings from slipping off the ends of the stick, wind a rubber band around each end of the stick, just outside of where the string is tied.)

HEDDLE BAR OR LEASH STICK

In plain tabby weave, the shed stick will make only alternate sheds. Some weavers, to speed the work, use a heddle bar (or leash stick) to make the other sheds.

Take a round wooden dowel, or other convenient-sized stick, long enough to go right across your weaving frame. Use two pieces of string. One piece is tied in a series of half hitches around the heddle bar. The other string forms a series of loops from the heddle bar around alternate warp threads (the ones that pass *under* the shed stick).

Alternatively, make separate, knotted loops of string from the heddle bar to alternate warp threads.

Heddle bar: placement of half hitches; loops formed with continuous string; separate knotted loops.

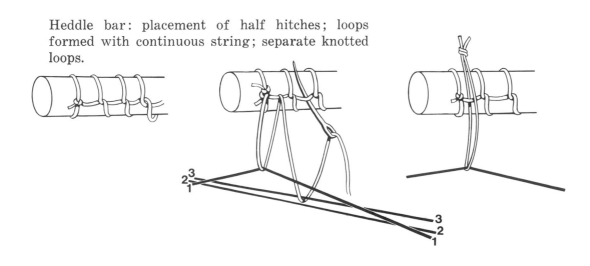

So with the heddle bar and the shed stick you can form the two different sheds that you need for tabby weave. If for some other weave—say, twill or blanket weave—you need a different series of sheds, you can leave the heddle bar lying on top of the warp; just push it out of the way, and it will not interfere with your manipulation of the warp threads. Then when you go back to tabby, you can use it again.

There's one difficulty: on a light frame, the upward pull of the heddle bar, instead of lifting half the warp threads, lifts the whole frame into the air. Some weavers fasten the frame to a table with C-clamps. Others feel the heddle bar is more trouble than it's worth, and never use it. You may like to give it a trial.

There is a way of attaching the heddle bar to a frame so that it can be operated conveniently. The bar is supported at its ends by two wooden arms, pivoted to the sides of the frame.

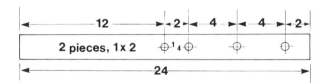

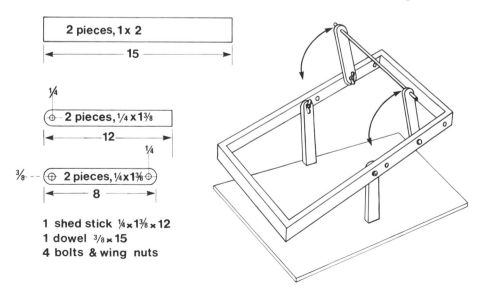

Frame with pivoted heddle bar.

1 shed stick ¼ x 1⅜ x 12
1 dowel ³⁄₈ x 15
4 bolts & wing nuts

When the bar is swung downward, the heddle loops hang loose; when it is pivoted upward, with its arms vertical, the heddles pull tight and lift their warp threads. There should be at least three pairs of pivot-holes. Start with the bar pivoted on the hole near the middle of the frame; as the work progresses, move it toward the top.

The diagram also shows a method of mounting a frame on two legs, to stand on the table at a convenient angle.

SHUTTLES

Instead of making the weft into a butterfly, some weavers prefer to wind it on a shuttle. You can buy shuttles of various shapes and sizes at weavers' supply stores, or you can make them. A

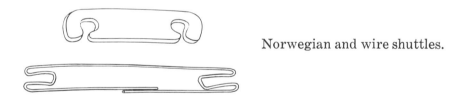

Norwegian and wire shuttles.

home-made wooden shuttle should have ends and edges sandpapered perfectly smooth. Balsa wood is easy to carve.

The Norwegian shuttle, which carries the weft on one side, has a straight, narrow edge, like a ruler, on the other side. It is much used in weaving narrow bands of fabric—in card weaving for example; it carries the weft and also serves as a handy tool for beating in.

For making the wire shuttle, use something as stiff as coat-hanger wire. The part where the two ends overlap will be bound with friction-tape. (In the diagram the joint is exposed to show its construction.)

Shuttles come in a wide range of sizes. The size you need de-

pends upon the size of the project. As a general rule, it should hold
at least enough weft to go ten times across the width of the warp.

To use the shuttle, unwind enough weft to make one shot; then
pass the shuttle through the shed.

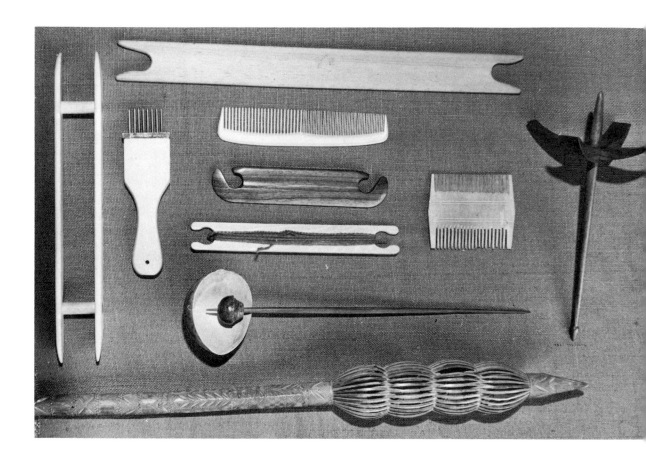

Weaving equipment: shuttles; spindles; beater; combs
for beating in; distaff. The dark-colored shuttle in the
center is a Norwegian shuttle; its lower edge is used for
beating in. The thin shuttle immediately below it shows
how the weft is wound on, ready for use.

CHAPTER 4

~~~~~~~~~~~~~~~~~~~~~~~~~~~~~~~~~~~

BEGINNING TO WEAVE

Most people like to begin by making a sampler that shows a number of different weaves on one web. If you are pleased with your initial effort, display it on the wall; it makes an interesting hanging, and you will often refer to it as you proceed to plan and carry out new projects.

WARPING THE FRAME

I suggest that you make the sampler about 7 inches wide. Before you put on the warp, tie a piece of fine wire to the first nail on the top of the frame and stretch it, parallel to the side of the frame, to the first nail on the bottom. Similarly tie another wire tightly from top to bottom between another opposed pair of nails, so that the two wires are 7 inches apart. These wires will help to keep the selvedge straight as you weave, and will be pulled out when the work is done.

For the warp, get some 3-ply wool or a heavy cotton yarn; 30 yards will be enough. For the weft, choose three colors of wool—

37

some 5-ply, some 3-ply; a total weight of 4 ounces should be ample. If you can get it, include 1 ounce of handspun wool; it gives an interesting texture variation.

Lay the tension stick close against the nails at the top of the frame.

Now take the ball of warp yarn and tie one end firmly to the top of the frame. Stretch the yarn around the top left-hand nail, around the corresponding nail at the bottom of the frame, and back to the top. This double thread gives a strong selvedge.

Then stretch the yarn from top to bottom, around the nails, so that the threads are parallel and 1/4 inch apart.

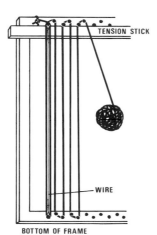

Warping the frame.

Finish off with a double thread between the two nails that support the second wire. Tie the yarn around the frame, and cut it off.

Don't strain the warp too tight; you should be able to take any thread by the middle and lift it about two inches without undue resistance.

Now here is an assortment of weaving techniques.

TWINING

Start with a row of twining, a special weave that spaces the warp threads evenly and prevents the weft from slipping on the warp.

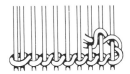
Twining.

Take a piece of weft three times the width of the web—in this instance, about 21 inches long. Fold it in half, and place the center against the bottom of the double warp thread at the extreme left. Weave it as shown above.

If this is properly done, the two halves of the weft thread not only cross between each two warp threads; they are *twisting* like a two-stranded rope.

After going around the double warp thread on the right, you have some surplus weft. Weave it back in the opposite direction, over one, under one, as far as it will go. When the loose ends become too short to handle, leave them hanging on the reverse of the web, that is, on the side away from you.

Beat in this row of twining with fork or comb; push the teeth through between the warp threads and press the weft down snugly against the bottom of the frame.

TABBY

Tabby, also called plain weave, passes the weft under one warp thread and over one, right across. Take about 6 feet of the weft you used for twining and make a butterfly. The shed stick has been inserted as described in Chapter 3, under one warp thread and over the next, right across the warp. Turn the shed stick on edge; the tension of the warp keeps it there, and you find half the warp threads are pressed down and half lifted up. Unravel about 15 inches of wool from the butterfly; pass the butterfly through the shed, leaving 3 inches of wool hanging on the side where you started.

Bubbling the weft.

Do *not* try to pull the weft straight. Make it form an arc (a "bubble" as weavers call it) about 2 inches high.

Darn the extra three inches of weft back into the warp, using the tabby weave; let the last little loose end project on the reverse. Now beat in the bubble, pressing it down to lie snugly against the row of twining.

The shed stick will not make the next shed that you need, so turn it down and let it lie flat. With your fingers, pick up every second warp thread, and pass the butterfly beneath it, forming a bubble as before. Note that the warp threads you lift this time are the ones previously pressed down by the shed stick.

Proceed in this way, back and forth, until you have only a few inches of weft remaining. Weave that in a little way from the edge, and let the end hang on the reverse.

Here are some practical hints for this first section of weaving.

1. Watch that, despite all precautions, you don't pull the weft tight as you make each shot, or the web will get narrower. (You can use a wooden yardstick for a shed stick, and so check the width of the web at all times.)

2. Check each shot as it is made, for correct under-and-over placement of the weft. It is easy to rectify an error at this stage, but difficult if you discover it after making a dozen more shots.

3. If you have to join on a new piece of weft of the same color at any time, do it by overlapping in the middle of a shot.

4. Beat with equal force all across, so that the rows remain all horizontal and parallel.

5. Find a comfortable posture. To leave the frame lying on the table, and bend over it, will give most people a backache. Try sitting, with the bottom of the frame on your lap, and the sides against the edge of a table.

When you have woven a strip of tabby about an inch wide, try the next weave.

BASKET WEAVE

Take two pieces of weft yarn together, side by side, going over-two-and-under-two warp threads.

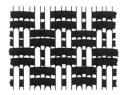

Two-over-two basket weave.

Basket weave can also be done with four weft yarns, going over-four-and-under-four warp threads.

BICOLORED WEFTS

Weave tabby with two weft yarns of different colors at the same time. Make one butterfly of the two yarns and pass them back and forth together. There's extra visual interest if the two yarns are of different thicknesses as well as different colors.

VERTICAL BARS

Take two wefts of different colors and weave one row of tabby with each color alternately: weft A alone for one shot; weft B alone for the next, and so on.

The diagram shows the wefts spaced out, for clarity; in practice, the weft must be well beaten in, and then it will produce vertical bars of A and B colors.

There is a slight technical problem with this weave. Each of the two wefts, being used alternately, always passes through the same shed, so does not go around the outside warp thread; this tends to produce an untidy-looking selvedge.

The remedy: as you finish one shot of weft (say, with yarn A), hang the butterfly over the edge of the frame, so that the yarn is stretched from the selvedge to the side-piece of the frame.

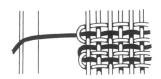 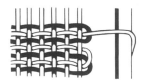

Making selvedges for vertical bar weave: weft passing over; weft passing under.

Now, when you take up weft B to weave the next shot, pass it over (or under) weft A in such a way that B is held out to the selvedge.

TWILL

Twill is a weave based predominantly on diagonal patterns. For a simple twill, weave over-*two*-and-under-*one*. To make the diagonal, move the pattern one warp thread to the right on each shot. If the first shot went under the 1st, 4th, and 7th warp threads, etc., the second shot goes under the 2nd, 5th, 8th warp threads, the third shot under the 3rd, 6th, 9th, etc.

You can also do a few rows of the same twill, sloped to the left.

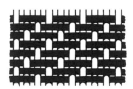
Twill weave.

SOUMAK

For soumak (pronounced soo′-mak) you take the weft over four warp threads, back under two, forward over four, back under two, and so on. When beaten in, soumak shows as a series of slightly sloping lines. You can make the slope run the same way on every shot; or you can make it slope the opposite way on each alternate shot, to give a herringbone effect.

Soumak: expanded to show the weave; after beating in—all sloped same way; after beating in—sloped alternate ways.

Do not try to weave many rows of soumak in succession: it would produce uneven spacing of the warp. If many rows of soumak are required, weave one or two rows of tabby following each row of soumak. Beat in well, and the soumak alone will be seen.

For variety of texture and pattern, the soumak rows can be woven from yarn that is thicker, and of a different color, than the tabby rows.

GHIORDES KNOT

The Ghiordes (pronounced yor'-deez) knot was originally developed for making pile rugs. It also serves to give textural variety to other kinds of weaving.

Cut about 30 pieces of thick yarn 4 inches long, to form the pile. Make the knots as follows:

a) Take a piece of cut yarn and lay it across two warp threads.

b) Bend the two ends down, under, and up between the two warp threads.

Making the Ghiordes knot.

c) Slide the knot down till it is snug against the previous row of weaving, and pull the ends to tighten it.

d) Make these knots right across the web.

e) Weave two rows of tabby, with yarn of the same color as the pile. Then put in another row of knots. Alternate one row of knots, two of tabby.

Continuous Weft

Instead of using precut pile, you can make a row of Ghiordez knots from one long piece of weft. On this row of knots, to make a uniform pile, you form a series of loops over a smooth stick or rod—the gauge.

1. Get a gauge of the right size to make the length of pile you want, and lay it across the warp at the point where you are to make the row of pile. Make a butterfly of weft.

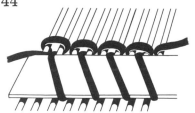

Making Ghiordes
knots from continu-
ous weft.

2. To form a knot, pass the weft *down* between the first two warp threads, right over both warp threads, *up* between the same two, and over the gauge. Then go *down* between warp threads 3 and 4, right over both warp threads, *up* between them and over the gauge again, and so on. Maintain an even tension on the weft on all the knots and loops.

3. Leave a short piece of weft hanging at the start of the row; weave it in when the row is completed.

4. There are two ways to finish off the row: (*a*) Cut with a sharp knife along the top of the gauge, to produce a row of pile. Beat in. (*b*) Withdraw the gauge and beat in the resulting row of loops.

CHAINING

Chaining is done without forming a shed; the weft passes around each warp thread. Practice chaining, at first, by working from left to right; most weavers find it easier that way. After you are familiar with the technique, you can do it in both directions.

1. Suppose you have finished a row of tabby, and are ready to begin chaining. To obtain a neat selvedge, start with the weft *underneath* the No. 1 warp thread. Now pass the weft all the way across, from left to right, underneath the warp.

(If you are beginning a fresh length of weft, darn the end of it into the warp about 2 inches, making sure that it passes under No. 1 warp thread.)

2. Form a small loop of weft, to the left of No. 1 warp thread and bend it over to the right.

3. Reach through this loop with thumb and finger; pull up a new loop of weft; similarly lay it over to the right. Pull the first loop tight.

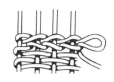

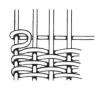 is part of a sequence with the other two.

Chaining: the first loop; the second loop; several
loops completed.

4. Reach through the new loop, again pick up a loop of weft.
Lay it over to the right, and tighten the second loop to grip it.

5. Continue like this right across the web. When you reach the
right selvedge, pass the end of the weft through the last loop, to
lock it, and darn the end back into the web. (This lock is essential;
without it, the whole row of chaining would unravel with one
pull on the end of the weft.)

Notes

Take care not to twist any of the loops in forming them, or you
will spoil the regular appearance of the chain.

Tighten all the loops with uniform tension, or the resulting
chain will have some "links" longer than others. On a widely
spaced warp, don't tighten the loops too much, or you will pull
the warp threads closer together.

Correctly done, this weave leaves the warp properly spaced;
indeed, you can use a row of chaining to restore correct spacing if,
in some other weave, the warp threads have become unevenly
spaced.

(If you are using a thick yarn for warp or weft, chaining may
spread the warp too far apart; then make each loop of the chain
over *two* warp threads instead of one; this preserves correct
spacing of the warp.)

Chaining can be used, instead of twining, to start or finish a
piece of work.

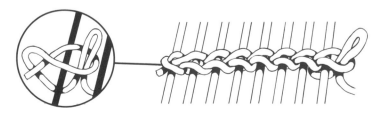

Starting a piece
of work with
chaining.

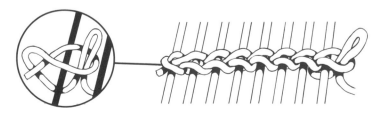 is the illustration at the bottom.

45

With thick yarn, chaining fills up a web quickly because each row covers as much warp as two rows of most weaves. But it uses quite a lot of yarn; a 7-inch row—varying to some extent with the thickness of yarn you use—will take up about 30 inches of yarn.

For this sampler, it will be sufficient to weave one or two rows of chaining; but if, in some other project, you wish to use chaining more extensively, always weave three rows of tabby between each two rows of chaining (with a contrasting weft yarn, if you like).

A useful variation: you need not chain all the way across the web. Weave part of a row in tabby, then chain for some distance; lock the last loop of the chain, and return to tabby. In this way, you can create pattern-areas of chain texture on a tabby background.

LOOPS

The method for making loops somewhat resembles that for the continuous-weft Ghiordes knot described above, except that for this purpose there is no need to make a knot on each two warp threads.

To make all loops the same size, use a gauge. A knitting needle would produce small loops; a half-inch dowel makes them larger; a ruler, larger still; you can cut a strip of smooth, stiff card to any width you choose. The gauge can be round or flat; it makes no difference to the result.

1. Before starting loops, weave two shots of tabby. Now throw a fresh shot of weft (as if for another row of tabby), but do not beat it in.

2. With a knitting needle, reach between the first and third warp threads; catch hold of the weft where it lies over the second warp thread, and pull it up toward you; slide the gauge under this raised loop of weft. Continue like this, picking up the weft at each point where it lies on top of a warp thread, and advancing the gauge till it lies right across the web. See that all loops lie with an even tension around the gauge.

3. Slide the gauge and its row of loops close to the completed tabby. *Leave the gauge inside the loops.*

4. Weave two more shots of tabby and beat them in close to the row of loops.

5. Now withdraw the gauge—carefully, so as not to pull some loops longer than others.

6. Again beat in both shots of tabby. Now the loops are firmly held, and with normal usage will not pull out.

Notes

Don't try to make two successive rows of loops; they won't hold properly. Always weave at least two shots of tabby after one row of loops before making another.

When making the next row of loops, pass the weft under alternate warps to those used for the previous row. (This should occur automatically, if you always have an *even* number of tabby rows between the rows of loops.)

You need not make loops all the way across. By making part of a row in loops and part tabby, you can inset areas of loops into a piece of ordinary flat weaving.

You will get best results by using a bulky, soft-twisted yarn for the loops, and a finer, harder-twisted yarn for the intervening rows of tabby.

THE GREEK KNOT

The Greek knot is a series of three half-hitches made one above another on each warp thread in turn. The weft may be wound in a butterfly, or on a small bobbin, or threaded in a bodkin. After completing the three half-hitches on one warp thread, the weft slants diagonally down to the next, to begin at the bottom of the new series of three half-hitches.

The half-hitches should be pulled fairly tight around each warp thread, and pressed down snugly one on the other. But *don't* pull

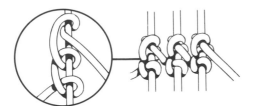

The Greek knot.

tightly on the diagonal "crossover" between one knot and the next; excess tension here pulls the warp threads together and narrows the web.

It is convenient to pass the weft clockwise around the warp threads when working from left to right; this leads the "crossover" smoothly to the next warp thread. For the same reason, it is advisable to pass the weft counterclockwise when working from right to left.

The Greek knot produces an interesting texture, something like a section of honeycomb, with a regularly spaced series of holes showing through the web. This effect is produced best with a fine weft yarn. With a close warp—say 8 threads to the inch—and fine weft well beaten in, the holes would be tiny. With a more widely spaced warp and coarser yarn, the holes are bigger.

You can get considerable variety from the Greek knot:

a) Use two half-hitches for a tighter, closer texture.

b) Use more than three half-hitches, to make larger openings.

c) Use wefts of different thicknesses in different areas for textural contrast.

d) Tie two warp threads together with each Greek knot.

e) Weave the Greek knot on the reverse side of the web; this will produce a ribbed effect on the face.

THE WRAPPED WARP

Instead of passing the weft back and forth across the web, you wind it around one warp thread (or, if the warp yarn is thin, wind around a small bundle of warp threads simultaneously).

Wind the weft round and round the first warp thread (or bundle); keep pushing the windings down, so that the turns lie

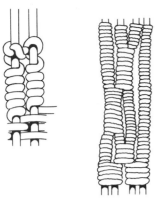

Wrapped warp technique, plain and complex.

snugly together. About every half-inch, tie a half-hitch, to secure the wrapping.

When you get as high as you wish to go, cross over to the next warp thread (or bundle) and wind downward on that. When you reach bottom, cross over and wind upward on the next warp thread (or bundle).

This straightforward technique produces a row of parallel wrapped warp threads with gaps between them. You can use the method in more elaborate ways. For example:

a) Wrap two groups separately for some distance, then combine them into one thicker group, and wrap that.

b) Wrap a group for some distance, then divide it into its constituent threads, and continue wrapping each separately.

There are great possibilities here for making a wide range of forms.

Wrapped warp can be very effective with a wrapping yarn that contrasts strongly in color and texture with the adjacent parts of the web. Silk, metal thread, etc., may provide the desired effect.

LENO LACE

In the weaves described so far, each shot is beaten in to lie close against the previous one (or, in the wrapped warp, the turns of wrapping lie close together) so that the entire warp is covered. In the leno lace technique, you leave fairly wide gaps between the wefts, so that sections of the warp are exposed, making a lacy, open-work texture. One or more wefts cross in this open area, and they are held in place by twists in the warp threads.

You can weave leno by manipulating the warp threads with your fingers and passing the weft on a butterfly, but it is easier to use a shed stick and a shuttle.

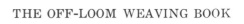

The sampler. *From bottom up*, fringe; twining; tabby; two-over-two basket weave; four-over-four basket weave; bicolored wefts; vertical bars; right-hand twill; left-hand twill; soumak; soumak on reverse side; Ghiordes knot; Ghiordes knot with tabby border; chaining; large loops; small loops; Greek knot; wrapped warp; tabby. (*Note.* For clarity, the different weaves have been separated by narrow bands of light-colored tabby.)

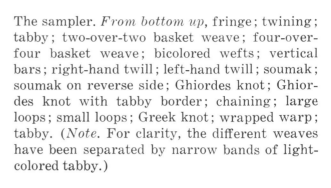

Handbag by Rose Naumann: various weaves, ornamented with feathers; shoulder strap is an inkle band.

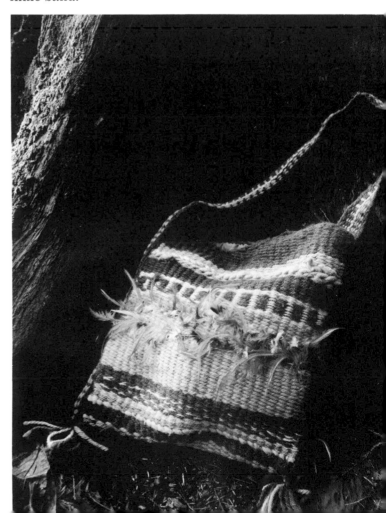

Before beginning the leno, complete a section of tabby and beat it in. If you are right-handed, it will be easier to begin the process at the right side of the web; so finish the tabby with your weft at the right side. If you are left-handed, proceed from the left.

1. Instead of making a shed in the ordinary way, pick up the second warp thread, cross it over the first, and insert the shed stick between them. The two warp threads are thus twisted between the last row of tabby and the shed stick; their tension makes a reverse twist above the shed stick.

2. Repeat the process with the next pair of warp threads; cross the fourth over the third and insert the shed stick. Continue in the same way across the web.

3. Turn the shed stick on edge and pass the shuttle. Don't pull the weft too tight—only just enough to make it straight. Remove the shed stick.

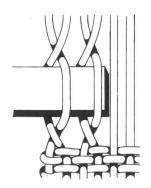 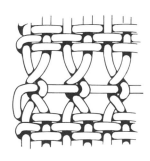

Leno lace: inserting the shed stick; the weft in place.

4. Don't try to beat in the weft; let it remain about ½ inch from the last row of tabby.

5. You can now weave another section of tabby, beginning about ½ inch from the row of leno you have just made; or you can weave two or three consecutive rows of leno, forming a wide band of the open-work pattern.

Note that leno is not effective with a warp of thick, soft yarn; where adjacent warp threads are twisted over each other, they seem to blend into one, and the textural interest is lost. A hard, tightly twisted yarn gives best results.

Two-over-two leno.

Variants of Leno Lace

You can vary the leno structure described above, especially if you are using a fine, closely spaced warp, by twisting two-over-two, or three-over-three.

An effective way to use leno is by not taking it all the way across the web; instead, you weave one or more rectangular blocks of leno, with tabby all around. Insert new wefts, where necessary, to make the blocks of tabby at the sides or in the middle of the web.

Notes

Because of the twisting involved, leno tends to cause considerable increase of warp tension. Plan ahead for this, so that you can reduce the tension by removing the tension stick or adjusting the frame; otherwise you may have difficulty in completing your sampler.

For best results, leno requires an attractive-looking warp yarn; for this reason, some weavers prefer to make a separate sampler for leno and for the warp bundle.

THE WARP BUNDLE

This is another open-work technique, different from leno. Finish off a section of tabby, weave the loose end of the weft back into the web, and beat in.

Take a piece of weft and, with two half-hitches, tie the first four warp threads together, about ½ inch from the edge of the tabby. Bundle the next four warp threads, carry the weft over, and tie them together with an overhand knot. Continue right across the web, keeping all the knots exactly the same distance from the edge of the tabby, and finish off with another two half-hitches.

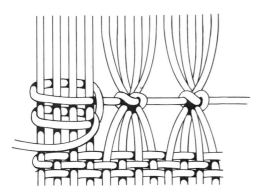

Warp bundles.

Then, about ½ inch from the knots, begin weaving another section of tabby.

(*Note*: the diagram shows the weft carried *in front of* the warp to form the half-hitches and knots. If you carry it *behind*, the bundles will be identical, but the knots will look slightly different on the face of the web.)

Warp bundling, like leno, can be carried right across the web, or can be inset in blocks, surrounded with tabby.

MAINTAINING CORRECT WIDTH

Here is a safeguard against the tendency to pull in the warp as you work, and so make the web progressively narrower. After you have woven about 3 inches, thread a piece of yarn or thin string through each side of the web—around the double outermost warp thread and the piece of wire—and knot it to the side of the frame. Use just enough tension on these two strings to keep the web the correct width. Repeat the procedure a few inches farther up; but this time put the strings, not around the outermost warp threads, but through the web, about an inch in from the edge; similarly tie to the side of the frame.

Alternate these two methods of tying all the way up the web.

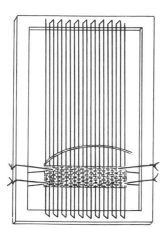

Tying the web to the frame.

FINISHING OFF

As you work toward the top of the frame, the warp becomes tight; remove the tension stick, and this will give you enough slack to continue.

Finish off with at least an inch of tabby, and one row of twining. Alternatively, you can secure the last row of tabby with needle and thread, using a diagonal overcast stitch. Each stitch ties the last two shots of weft together, and also crosses over one warp thread.

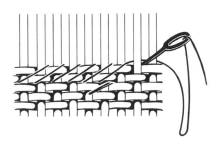

Finishing off with needle and thread.

Remove the ties between the sampler and the sides of the frame. Untie the ends of the warp and the two wires. With a small screwdriver, or a closed pair of scissors, carefully lift each loop off the nails. Pull out the wires from the selvedges. Now you have several possible ways of preparing the sampler for display.

1. If you have an attractive-looking warp, slide wooden dowels, or metal rods, through the top and bottom loops.

2. If the warp is not particularly attractive, fold over the top and bottom loops and sew them to the reverse of the sampler. In the process, double over a little of the web, and leave top and bottom openings wide enough to slide dowels through.

3. A piece of tape or binding is stitched by machine to the ends of the sampler, on the face or right side, at the edge of the weaving. The tape is turned over and hemstitched to the reverse side of the piece, leaving an opening wide enough for the dowels to go through.

4. Clamp each end of the sampler between two slats of nice-looking wood, held together by small nails. Alternatively, you can

wrap the slats, before fastening them to the sampler, with one of the yarns you used in the weaving.

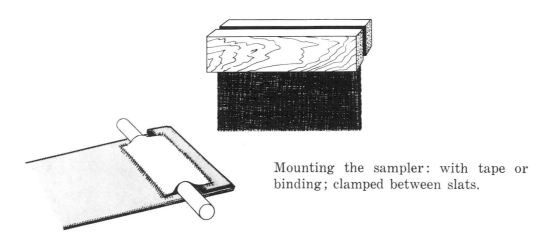

Mounting the sampler: with tape or binding; clamped between slats.

STRIPES AND CHECKS

You can create vertical stripes by setting up a warp of several colors and using a plain weft of the same thickness as the warp. This is called a 50-50 weave, and will show the colors of the warp.

Horizontal stripes are made by changing the weft colors on a plain warp. Horizontal stripes woven on a striped warp will make a check pattern.

A HANDBAG

Set up a warp 12 inches wide and 28 inches long, with 5-ply wool or heavy cotton. For weft, get three colors of wool, some 3-ply, some 5-ply; 8 ounces will be ample. As with the sampler, also get, if you can, 1 ounce of hand-spun wool.

The main piece of the bag is woven in stripes, each displaying a different color or texture. Vary the width of the stripes according to your taste. Proceed in much the same way as you did for the sampler, finishing with twining or with an overcast stitch.

The Shoulder Strap

The shoulder strap is made in two halves, each 28 x 2 inches. Set up two warps, each 2 inches wide, the full length of the frame, keeping them well apart, so that you have room to work with your hands between them.

Weave each strap in the same way as the body of the handbag. (Alternatively, if you have already mastered card weaving or inkle weaving, you can use one of those techniques to make the strap in one piece, 56 inches long.)

Finishing the Bag

The two 2-inch strips serve to join the front and back of the bag as well as to form the shoulder strap.

1. Before assembling the bag, pull out the wires from the selvedges. Turn over the warp loops at the ends of the main piece and the straps, and sew them to the reverse with an overcast stitch. Loose ends of wool hanging from this side of the fabric should be trimmed to $\frac{1}{4}$ inch. Press the fabric under a damp cloth.

2. On the reverse of the main piece sew a lining of some smooth fabric.

3. Fold the main piece in half, wrong side out, and sew in the strap halves with an overcast stitch.

4. Join the strap halves at the shoulder with a metal ring or buckle.

5. Press the whole bag again after assembling.

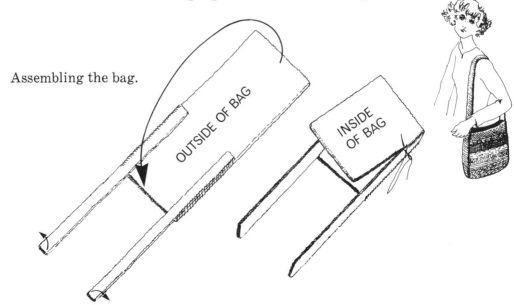

Assembling the bag.

OUTSIDE OF BAG

INSIDE OF BAG

CHAPTER 5

~~~~~~

SUGGESTIONS AND IDEAS

You are now ready to utilize the techniques described in the previous chapters and create useful, attractive articles, using your own initiative in the choice of yarns and materials.

CUSHION COVERS

Because a cushion has a substantial thickness, you will not get accurate results by just measuring the width and doubling it. Measure right around the cushion with a tape measure in both directions to find the size of cover you need.

If your frame is big enough, and the cushion small enough, you can weave the cover in one piece, to be folded in half and sewn up. On the frame described in Chapter 3 (28 x 20 inches) you could make a one-piece cover, 28 x 14 inches, for a cushion 14 x 14 inches.

Materials

Two-ply wool makes a good warp. For weft, you can use a wide variety of materials—different colors and thicknesses of wool, 57 strips of leather, strips of fur, all chosen to harmonize with your other furnishings.

Patterns

For cushion covers, you can try something a little more complex than the plain stripes you used in the sampler and handbag. You can also use a wide variety of textures, including areas of loops and pile. Cushions can also be ornamented with tassels or fringes.

HASSOCKS

You can make a good-sized hassock with four sides 12 inches high and 23 inches wide. The top and bottom are 23 inches square. A hassock must stand a good deal of strain, so use a strong cotton rug warp, and weave tightly.

For extra strength, use a square of leather for the bottom, instead of woven fabric. For a different texture, make the top of tapestry. (See Chapter 6.)

A LARGE BAG

Here is an application of twining by which you can make a packsack or a big handbag. It is a very flexible technique and, by finding the correct base to work on, you can make a bag in any dimensions you choose.

As an example, suppose you are going to work on the back of a wooden kitchen chair.

Get some strong rug warp—10/5 linen or 6-ply cotton—and make a horizontal loop of it around the sides of the chair-back, near the top. Tie the ends tightly together.

To make a bag 15 inches deep, cut some pieces of warp yarn 32 inches long. Double each piece; fasten it at its center with a snitch knot to the horizontal loop, and let the ends hang down. Space these hanging warp threads 4 to the inch all the way around.

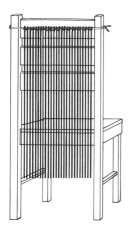
Setting up warp for the large bag.

Now take some weft yarn; begin twining at the top, and keep on twining round and round, working down toward the bottom. Here's a practical hint for doing continuous twining. Arrange your first piece of weft so that one end of it runs out before the other; add a new piece by overlapping about an inch with that end; a little further, similarly add another new piece as the longer end runs out. Keep alternating in this way so that both ends never run out together.

Change the color of your weft from time to time, to make a series of horizontal stripes; or twine with two different colors at once.

Don't twine right to the bottom of the warp; leave about an inch of each warp thread uncovered. Slip the work off the chair-back, turn it inside-out and, to close the bottom of the bag, square-knot the opposite warp threads together.

For a shoulder strap, sew on buckles at the top and use a leather strap; sew on an inkle-woven or card-woven band, or a braided cord. Ornament the bottom of the bag, if you wish, with tassels or a fringe.

That's the basic procedure. To vary the size of the bag, simply use a bigger or smaller object as a base for the weaving—say, a picture frame, your weaving frame, etc.—and vary the length of the down-hanging warp threads.

LAMPSHADES

Here are two procedures for weaving lampshades.

Leno

Get a wire lampshade frame (the cylindrical shape is easiest

Four cushion covers. No. 1, twining; No. 2, tabby weave and strips of fur; No. 3, tapestry in triangular pattern; No. 4, various textures of wool, including some handspun.

Large handbag, by Anne Robinson. Warp: camel hair. Weft: handspun wool of various thicknesses, and suede strips. (Also illustrated: a shuttle and a spindle.)

Lampshade, by Linda Wills. Horsehair warp and weft; leno technique.

for a first attempt). Set up a warp, stringing it between the top and bottom wire circles of the frame. Weave a row of twining or chaining at the top to keep the warp evenly spaced, then weave the rest of the shade in leno.

Woven Grass

This method produces a very attractive lampshade featuring stems of dried grass, seed-heads, cedarwood fibers, thin leaf-fronds, or similar nature objects.

a) Get a cylindrical wire lampshade frame and cover it with parchment.

b) Set up a warp on your weaving frame exactly as wide as

the lampshade is high. Use a thin, white, good-looking yarn for warp, because it will be clearly seen on the finished shade.

c) Use your grass and other nature materials as weft. Don't crowd it; let each piece stand alone, without any crushing or overlapping. The height of the web must be exactly the same as the measurement around the lampshade.

d) Carefully remove the web and put it around the lampshade so that the warp threads are horizontal and the grass stems vertical. Knot the ends of the warp yarns. If the weaving tends to slip down, fix it to the parchment with a spot of white glue here and there.

WALL HANGINGS

Most weavers, having mastered the various techniques described elsewhere in this book, want to apply them creatively; this trend in modern weaving finds, perhaps, its freest expression in the creation of wall hangings.

You can select size, shape, color, design to express your own personality, emotions, and taste. You can use materials that relate to your own surroundings, your own special interests. If you are a hiker, you may collect lichens, mosses, and twigs from the trees; if you live near the sea, you may collect shells, driftwood, and pieces of rope washed ashore. If you live in the city, you might want to use glass, plastics in various forms and colors, metal rods or wires, and the synthetic fibers.

One advantage of weaving on a frame is that you can use fragile materials, because your work will not be bent or rolled up as it would be on a mechanical loom.

Again, because a wall hanging does not have to fulfill a practical purpose, you can use a widely spaced warp, and so show the beauty of warp and weft to full advantage. You can show the texture of a handspun yarn; by weaving in different spacings— here close together, there wide apart—you can create lovely effects.

One very important point: take great care in selecting the rod on which your hanging will be mounted. It is not good enough to use a piece of wooden dowel! The rod must be a perfect extension, an integral part, of the total work. It might be a carefully polished piece of wood, a bamboo pole, or a well-formed tree branch.

As for the bottom of the hanging, it is often advisable to use a rod considerably heavier than the one at the top, to make the work hang well. If this rod is suitable in appearance, it can be left in sight; otherwise, sew it behind the web and finish off as shown on page 55.

A DOUBLE HANGING

You can make a hanging in two "levels," with a plain background showing through an openwork front.

Instead of looping your warp yarn over nails, wind it right over the top of the frame, down the back, under the bottom, over the top again, and so on.

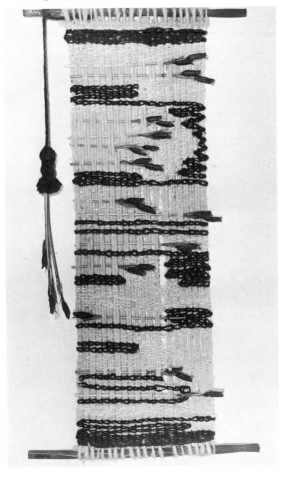

Wall hanging, by Vee Elder. Warp: linen. Weft: linen, Queen Anne's lace, and fern fronds.

Wall hanging by Rose Naumann. Warp: handspun wool. Weft: nubby rayon bouclé, handspun wool, and iris seedpods. The end loops of the warp are passed around wrought-iron rods.

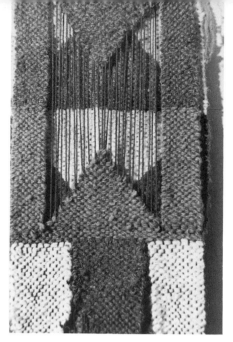

Wall hanging, by Yvonne D'Hont. Warp and weft: handspun linen. Note the wrapped-warp technique in the round openings.

Double wall hanging, by Jo-Anne Ryburn.

On the back, use a fairly plain weave in one or two colors, or in two shades of one color. Use a wide-spaced tabby, to cover the ground quickly.

Weave an open pattern on the front, using colors and materials that contrast well with the background. (While you work, put a sheet of cardboard between the two levels, so that your weft does not get entangled with the wrong set of warp threads.)

A collapsible or adjustable frame is best for this project. When you are finished, loosen the joints and dismantle the frame; or slide the top and bottom of an adjustable frame closer together; then you can easily take off the finished hanging.

To display the double hanging, put dowel rods, or 1- x 2-inch sticks inside the top and bottom turnovers, to hold the back and front webs a little way apart.

RUGS

Rugs can be made in one piece, up to the maximum dimensions of your frame; yet even with a small frame, you can still produce perfectly good rugs, by making 1-foot or 18-inch squares that will be sewn together to make up the required size.

There are many rug-making techniques; the one described here uses the Ghiordes knot which you made on the sampler. (This kind of knotted rug is also called a rya rug.)

Materials

A rug must stand heavy wear, so use the tough yarns sold specially for rug-making. For warp, use 10/5 linen or 6-cord cotton. For pile, use a good 4-ply or 5-ply rug wool; some silk and linen can also be used for variety of texture. The rug also includes many rows of tabby weave; the yarn for this may be fine or coarse, but it must be strong and durable. You can, if you like, use the same rug wool that forms the pile.

(For these tabby rows, some weavers use strips of cloth, such as old bedsheets dyed to the correct color, torn into 1½-inch strips, folded to ½-inch width, woven and beaten in.)

Precut Pile

One popular method is to cut the pile before you begin to weave. For this, a special gauge may be used, a stick with a slot cut down one side. Wind the wool smoothly on the gauge, with just enough tension to make the turns lie evenly, but not enough to stretch the yarn; cut down the slot with a sharp knife or a razor blade.

If you don't want to buy a gauge, you can cut a strip of cardboard to the width you want (e.g., 2 inches wide to make pieces 4 inches long), wind the wool around it, and cut down one edge with a pair of scissors.

Cut plenty of pile, in whatever colors you are going to use, before you start to weave. The work goes faster if you can get into a steady rhythm, without constantly having to stop to cut more pile.

I suggest that for your first rug you cut the pile in 4-inch pieces; this, on the finished rug, will give a pile standing about 1½ inches high.

WARPING THE FRAME

Apply the warp 6 or 8 to the inch. See that you have an even number of warp threads, because the knotting process uses them in pairs, and you don't want an odd one left over.

If you want fringes on the ends of the rug, you have two choices:

a) If you have length to spare on your frame, allow extra length on the warp—say 4 to 6 inches on both ends—so that, when the weaving is done, the projecting warp ends can be cut to serve as fringes.

b) If your frame is not long enough for method (*a*), make the warp just long enough for the body of the rug, and add the fringes afterward, by one of the methods described in Chapter 12.

Remember also that the warp is going to tighten up as the work progresses; allow 1 inch per foot. There will also be a shrinkage in width of about 1 inch per foot as the knotting draws the warp threads closer together.

BASIC RUG WEAVES

The rya rug has many rows of Ghiordes knots which form the pile, give texture, thickness, and warmth, and which also form the pattern.

Between the rows of knots are rows of tabby weave, not visible on the finished rug (except at the ends and, in one technique mentioned later, down the edges) but essential to hold the rug together.

The proportion of knots to tabby may be varied according to the length of pile and the thickness of rug you want. With 4-inch pile pieces, one row of knots to four of tabby would give a close-packed, upstanding pile. At the other extreme, with 6-inch pile pieces, and with eight rows of tabby between each two rows of knots, you have a shaggy pile that tends to lie flat.

Let's begin.

1. Weave a row of twining to give a firm edge to the rug.

This will be at the bottom of the frame if you don't want warp-end fringes; if you do want these fringes, begin the appropriate distance up the warp.

2. Weave 1 inch of tabby, beating in firmly.

3. Make a row of Ghiordes knots, using two or three pieces of yarn for each knot. This makes each row of knots wider, and speeds the work.

For pure color, make each knot with two or three pieces of the same yarn. For a richer color effect, use two or more different hues of the same tone value; thoroughly mix the pile pieces and knot three together for each tuft.

4. Weave four more rows of tabby. (The knots tend to group the warp threads by twos, but don't make the mistake of doing basket weave, over-two-and-under-two. Take your weft over and under individual warp threads; that makes a stronger rug.)

5. Continue with one row of knots, four of tabby, always beating in firmly, till you get near the top.

6. When you have about 2½ inches to go, make a slight change in the knots. The way the knots have been formed so far would tend to make them all lie one way, toward the bottom of the rug. To make some of the pile lie over the top end of the rug, alternate the knots in the last two or three rows; make half of them upward, half downward.

7. Finish off with an inch of tabby and another row of twining.

8. Lift the warp off the nails (or, if you are using a Salish frame, remove the floating loom-bar). If you are not making fringes, turn the loops under and sew them to the back of the rug.

9. Sew a strip of cotton rug binding under each end. If a strong warp has been used, there is no need for any overall backing.

VARIATIONS

Flat-Edged Rug

Some weavers like to have a 1-inch strip of tabby, not only at the ends, but down both sides of the rug as well. To make this, proceed as follows.

1. Begin as described above, with a row of twining; but to weave the 1-inch strip of tabby, use *two* shuttles or butterflies of weft yarn, weaving one shot with each of them in turn. Finish off the strip of tabby with one weft shuttle on each side of the web.

2. Put in the first row of knots, starting and finishing 1 inch from the edges.

3. On each side, weave a 1-inch row of tabby in from the edge to the knots, and out to the edge again. (This is necessary to keep the work even all the way across.)

4. Then weave four rows of tabby, using each shuttle alternately (i.e., two rows with each shuttle). Again you end up with one shuttle on each side of the web.

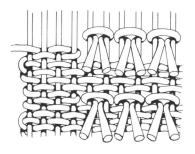

Weaving flat-edged rug.

5. Put in the next row of knots.

6. Continue like this till you reach the top. Finish off with a 1-inch tabby strip right across, as in the previous method.

Continuous Weft

You can form Ghiordes knots by the continuous-weft process described earlier. The whole rug can be made of uncut loops formed in this way; you can cut all the loops to form a pile; or you can use some areas of loops and some of cut pile, to give variety of texture.

You can also use the continuous-weft method with two or three weft yarns simultaneously (of the same or mixed colors). A big-eyed needle will carry three weft yarns at once. Many weavers find the needle faster than using a butterfly.

Uneven Pile

The methods described so far produce a pile of uniform height. To make an uneven pile, you can cut the pile pieces of irregular length to start with; one way is by winding the wool over your hand instead of on a parallel-sided gauge. Mix the pieces well before use; this will produce a random variation of pile-height all over the rug.

You may want a controlled variation of pile height. Suppose, for example, you have a geometric pattern in black and white; you want the pile in the black areas to be half an inch higher than in the white. Then make two gauges and cut the white pile pieces 1 inch shorter than the black. (1-inch difference in the cut pieces makes $\frac{1}{2}$-inch difference in height when they are doubled and knotted.)

You can give certain areas a rounded contour by trimming the pile with scissors after it is in place.

You can also make rows of loops with a continuous weft, as described above, but *without* a gauge, so that some are longer than others. The loops can be cut or left uncut.

Pile-Warp Relationship

When experimenting with different kinds and arrangements of pile, bear these points in mind. If the pile yarn is too thin, the knots will squeeze the warp threads too close together, and the rug will buckle; if the pile yarn is too thick, gaps will show.

COLORS AND PATTERNS

So much for the technique of rug-knotting. You will probably not want to make a plain rug, all of one color, so it is necessary to plan your pattern before you begin.

If you are making a rug in sections, for sewing together, you can make a repetitive pattern (i.e., each section has the same pattern). You can get considerable variation by using different arrangements of the pattern unit.

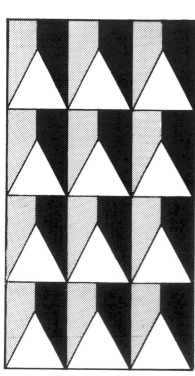

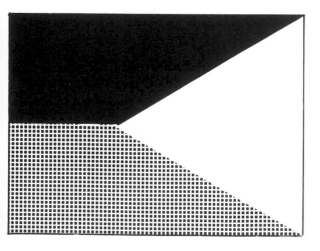

Variations of repetitive pattern.

Alternatively, you can have an overall pattern, and draw a scale plan to show exactly what part of it goes in each section. Fasten this plan behind the frame, to guide you as you work.

When making a rug in sections, pay careful attention to the way the pile lies on each section; the pile must lie the same way right across the rug. Decide which way the pile is to lie before you weave; make your plan, mark each section with an arrow to indicate pile direction, and weave accordingly.

Color Changes

To change from one solid color to another, just change the color of the pile pieces you are using. (The color of the warp and the tabby rows can remain the same throughout.)

To make bicolored or multicolored areas, thoroughly mix pre-cut pile pieces of the chosen colors, and knot them in at random.

To make a gradual change from one color to another, use the multiple-pile technique. Suppose you want to change from green to blue. Begin by using 3 pile pieces of green to each knot. At the point where you want the color change to start, switch to 2 green and 1 blue. A little farther on, use 1 green and 2 blue, and eventually 3 blue pieces per knot.

JOINING RUG SECTIONS

If you have woven the rug in sections, you can sew them together with strong linen thread on the reverse side. An alternative method is to weave a half-inch strip of flat tabby all around each section. (The way to make such a flat border was described earlier in this chapter.) To join the sections, overlap these edge strips and machine-stitch them together.

CHAPTER 6

TAPESTRY TECHNIQUES

Tapestry-weaving, sometimes described as "painting in wool," is the only weaving process to have acquired the status of a major art. Louis XIV of France patronized the famous Aubusson tapestry works. Great painters such as Raphael and Rubens drew cartoons for the tapestry weavers of Europe.

Tapestry, in historic times, served primarily as a wall decoration. In churches, it provided religious instruction and inspiration during an era when few people could read. In kings' palaces, great public buildings, and noblemen's castles, tapestries served to record the history, and to gratify the pride, of monarchs, of nations, and of aristocratic families. Tapestry also functioned, more prosaically, as insulation for cold walls, and as a screen against cold drafts.

Tapestry is the most creative of textile processes; it cannot be carried out by power-looms, but must be done by hand. There has been, in recent years, a great revival of interest in tapestry. Nowadays, most weavers sooner or later try tapestry, and many of them find it the most interesting, most satisfying of weaving techniques.

71

There is nothing difficult about tapestry: it is essentially a weft-faced fabric (i.e., with the warp completely covered), bearing a design, pictorial, geometric, or abstract, in several colors.

The basic weave for tapestry is tabby. Each tapestry consists of many different colored areas, each of which is woven with its own different-colored weft. Methods of joining these colored shapes are explained later in this chapter.

YARNS FOR TAPESTRY

In most tapestries, the warp is completely covered. This requires that the weft be well beaten in, so the warp yarn must be strong to stand the strain. A smooth size-9 cotton, a cotton seine twine, or a cable twine, makes a good warp; so does hard-twisted wool worsted. Warp color is not usually important, except in some modern designs where part of the warp is left uncovered; then, of course, warp color and texture must be chosen for their contribution to the overall design.

The 2-ply and 3-ply wools are popular for weft. A fairly thin handspun wool gives a different texture; so do cotton, silk, and rayon. Gold and silver thread can be used for color highlights.

SHAPING THE COLOR AREAS

Now let us see how to create the color areas that form a tapestry design. There are several methods.

Vertical Slit

Suppose you are weaving two adjoining color areas; on the left, brown, and on the right, white. Weave the brown weft thread from the left to the dividing line; then turn it and weave back toward the left.

Similarly, weave the white weft thread from right to left, up to the adjacent warp thread; turn around that thread and weave back toward the right.

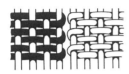 The vertical slit.

This method makes a sharp break between the two colors, but it leaves a vertical slit in the web. For some purposes—for example, a wall hanging—the slit may serve as a decorative element of the design; then you can leave it open. But if the slit is too long, say, more than 3 inches—sew the sides together, on the back of the web, with a neutral-colored thread.

Interlocking

In the interlocking technique, the two weft threads meet, and are interlocked between two warp threads; then they are turned back and woven in the opposite direction again. (By contrast, in the slit technique, the two different-colored threads stop just short of touching each other.)

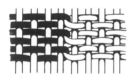 Interlocking.

This method obviously works best when the two color areas are being advanced, shot for shot, at an equal rate. Interlocking produces a stronger fabric than does the slit; but there is inevitably a slight blurring of the two colors where they meet. For some designs, of course, this is desirable.

Dovetail

Bring the two different-colored weft threads from opposite directions, and make them encircle the same warp thread before they turn back.

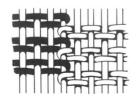 Dovetail.

This method, too, produces a strong, unbroken fabric; but the warp thread that serves as turning point has twice as much weft on it as the others; so, if the dovetail is continued very far in one direction, it produces a bulge at this point, and the rows of weft will not lie straight when they are beaten in. For some kinds of work, this would be a disadvantage.

Diagonal Patterns

Diagonal patterns are made by moving the color change more or less rapidly to right or left on succeeding rows of weft.

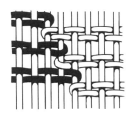

Diagonal color change: slit method; dovetail method.

As you see from the diagram, you do not produce a true diagonal line, but a stepped color change which, seen from a distance, looks like a diagonal.

Note that, in working diagonals, it is not necessary to proceed, shot for shot, at exactly the same rate in both color areas; indeed, it is easier to weave one of the color areas an inch or two ahead, and then catch up with the other.

Hatching

As we saw above, interlocking and dovetailing produce a slight color-blending between two adjacent areas; but this is not enough where a gradual color transition is required, or a blending of two colors over a width of several inches. For this purpose, you weave narrow lines of one color right into the adjoining color area.

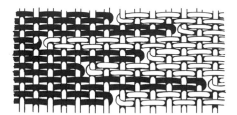

Hatching.

Two Important Rules

As I mentioned above, it is often necessary—as in weaving diagonals—to weave one shape first and then work on the adjoining shapes. There are two principles to bear in mind.

1. Weave decreasing shapes first. "Decreasing shapes" are color areas that become narrower in the direction you are working, that is, from bottom to top of the frame.

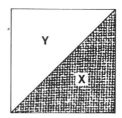 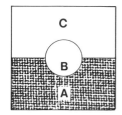

Decreasing shapes.

On the left, X is the decreasing shape (it gets narrower as you work from bottom to top), so you would weave X first. On right, A is the decreasing shape in the bottom of the pattern (its two side portions grow narrower from bottom to top at right and left of the central circle) ; in the top part, B is the decreasing shape.

If you break this rule, and weave increasing shapes first, you run into difficulties trying to weave the last narrow corners of the decreasing shapes.

2. Usually—even when working on a decreasing shape—don't weave one shape too far ahead before bringing adjoining shapes up to the same level. (To get too far ahead with one part of the design would tend to distort the spacing of the warp threads.)

Navajo child weaving tapestry in Monument Valley, Utah. (*Photo: Ulli Steltzer*)

A TAPESTRY SAMPLER

The photograph shows a tapestry sampler, to be woven in two contrasting colors, that will provide practice in the above-mentioned techniques.

Draw a copy of this design, enlarging it to the dimensions you intend to use. A convenient size would be 18 to 24 inches long; the exact measurements will depend on the size of your frame. But don't make the design itself run the entire length of your warp; leave about 2 inches empty at both ends for a turnover border.

Bearing this in mind, prepare a full-size plan of the sampler, with all color areas outlined, on a sheet of strong paper. Fasten this cartoon into your weaving frame, behind the warp. It will guide you as you work.

Alternatively, if you are good at freehand drawing, you can mark the design right onto the warp threads, with a thick marker pencil, felt pen, or India ink.

Preparing to Weave

Tape a tension stick near the top of the frame, and over it apply the warp—cotton seine twine—6 threads to the inch, with a double thread at each selvedge.

Prepare your weft yarn by winding lengths of the two colors into butterflies. Another convenient way to handle the warp is by winding the yarns criss-cross on small cardboard squares; cut a slit in the card near one corner, and pull the yarn through this when you need to anchor it, so that it won't all unravel.

Yarn wound on cardboard.

Tapestry sampler in black and white, designed to utilize all techniques described in this chapter.

Weaving the Sampler

1. Before you begin to weave, make a shed and insert a strip of cardboard 1 inch wide, and as long as the width of the warp. Above the card, weave 8 rows of tabby loosely, with the same yarn that you used for the warp. (Tight weaving will pull in the warp, and make the web too narrow.) Beat in well.

Now pull out the cardboard. Take another piece of warp yarn and, immediately below the bottom row of tabby, tie the warp threads together in pairs, using double half-hitches.

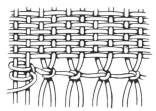

Tying warp threads in pairs.

This must be done before you weave any farther. It prevents the subsequent beating from driving the weft downward on the warp. This strip of tabby will serve, after the sampler is finished, as a border to be turned under, without too much bulk.

2. Weave the design according to the instructions previously given. Remember always to bubble the weft, as in other kinds of weaving, and to beat in well.

If it is necessary to join on a new length of weft, don't do it at the selvedge. Overlap the new piece with the end of the first one, for about an inch, somewhere near the center of a row. Any short loose ends can be left hanging on the reverse.

3. To maintain an even width, proceed as described for the weaving sampler in Chapter 4. As every inch or two of the tapestry is completed, tie it out to the sides of the frame. Don't trust your eye: measure the width of the tapestry from time to time with a yardstick. For best results, vary the placement of the ties; the first one goes through the web just inside the selvedge; the second goes through 1 inch from the selvedge; the third is close to the selvedge again, and so on.

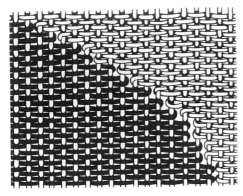

Forming a circle.

4. The circle is one of the more difficult shapes to produce in tapestry. You cannot make a perfectly round circle, in fact. It must be built up of a series of straight lines and diagonals of varying steepness.

5. At the top, weave another 8 rows of tabby, as you did at the bottom, and similarly tie the warp threads together in pairs.

Finishing and Mounting

Take the tapestry off the frame. For extra firmness at top and bottom you can, if you like, machine-stitch two or three times across the last one or two rows of tabby. On tapestry, some weavers prefer not to make fringes of the warp yarn, because it is usually not particularly attractive in appearance. So turn over the tabby borders, top and bottom; then mount the sampler for hanging by one of the methods described for the sampler in Chapter 4. If you do wish to make fringes, follow the instructions in Chapter 12.

ORIGINAL DESIGNS

After completing the sampler, you will want to make some tapestries to your own design. You may find inspiration in nature —from the shape of a seashell, a rock formation, a clump of tree-roots, the pattern formed by pebbles on a beach, or by water plants on the surface of a pool.

You might sketch a tree, then a group of trees; combine and re-combine the shapes, joining, overlapping, to bring out one definite, strongly colored shape against a pale background.

Work at your sketches till you have a satisfying composition that is simple enough to be woven with ease. Then make your full-size cartoon.

In planning a tapestry, it's important to remember that, since the design is formed by the weft, it is easier to weave horizontal lines than vertical ones.

If your design contains many strong vertical lines, you should plan to weave the tapestry sideways; give the design a quarter-turn before attaching it to your frame, so that most of the strong lines run at right-angles to the warp. When the tapestry is completed, it will be hung with the warp horizontal and the weft vertical. A tapestry thus woven sideways requires some additional care in hanging; stitch a strip of firmly woven cloth to the top, to make a stronger edge for hanging.

TAPESTRY PROJECTS

Book Cover

To make a book cover, open the book flat, lay it on a sheet of paper, and draw around it. This gives you the dimensions for the tapestry that will form the outside of the cover.

Make your own design for the tapestry, choosing colors and motifs appropriate to the book.

Weave the tapestry. Line it with some strong, plain fabric, joining the lining to the tabby hems at the top and bottom. With the same lining, make pockets into which the covers of the book can be slipped.

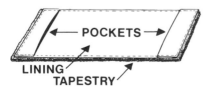

Plan of tapestry book cover.

UNCONVENTIONAL MATERIALS

Mrs. Jenina Jacobov kindly offered the following suggestions for unusual tapestry materials. They create effects markedly different from those attainable with ordinary tapestry yarns;

they provide the additional satisfaction of utilizing materials that might otherwise have been wasted.

Metal Foil

You can use many kinds of metal foil, in natural aluminum or any other color, with a glossy or matte surface. Foil that has been crumpled and partly straightened so that it retains innumerable small creases will have a different reflective effect from foil that is smooth. Here are three techniques.

1. Foil Strings

a) Take a piece of thick, fairly stiff string, and a piece of foil a little wider than the length of the string.

b) Lay the string at one corner of the foil, and roll the foil around it.

c) Finally, twist the two ends of the foil in opposite directions, to prevent it from unrolling.

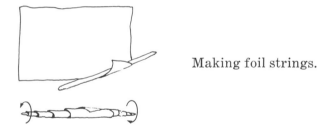

Making foil strings.

Foil strings can be used as weft in your tapestry. You can produce them in a variety of thicknesses by varying the size of the string used as a core.

2. Foil Cocoons

To make a tapering, cigar-shaped form, use a rolled-up wad of paper as a core.

a) Take a square of paper. For a fairly thin cocoon, use thin paper, like a paper napkin; for thicker cocoons, use larger sheets of thicker paper, such as a paper towel. Fold the paper twice, to make four thicknesses; fold it diagonally into a triangle; then roll it up, beginning with the long side of the triangle.

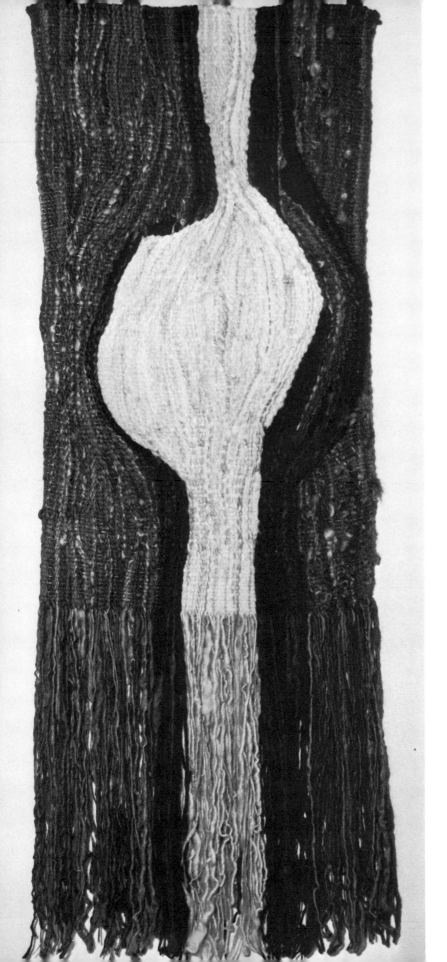

Tapestry, by Susan Cox.
Note that this design,
with its strong vertical
lines, was woven side-
ways on the frame, with
warp running in the
shorter dimension, i.e.,
horizontally in the photo.
The handspun-wool weft
runs vertically.

TAPESTRY TECHNIQUES

Tapestry, "Rising Moon," by a student at University of British Columbia School of Education. Handspun-wool weft.

Tapestry book cover, by Hilda Gerson.

Tapestry hassock, by Rose Nau-mann. The top is woven in the slit technique, with the edges of the slits sewn together.

Tapestry wall hanging, by a student at the University of British Columbia School of Education.

Found-object tapestry, by Sally Thurpie, using as warp the branch of a date palm.

Detail of tapestry, by Jenina Jacobov, incorporating foil strings, foil cocoons, and horsehair bundles.

Making foil cocoons.

b) Wrap this cigar-shaped roll of paper in foil, much as you did with the string. Twist the ends of the cocoon.

3. Big Cocoons

To make big, thick cocoons, use an inner wrapping of fabric before applying the foil.

a) Take a three-cornered piece of cloth, made by cutting diagonally across a square; lay it on the core material you want to use—fabric scraps, cotton batting, etc. Roll it up into a fat cigar-shape, beginning at the right-angle corner of the cloth.

b) Wind thread around the cocoon to hold it firm.

c) Cut a piece of foil to a similar triangular shape, but a couple of inches bigger than the piece of cloth. Place the cloth-wrapped cocoon near the right-angle corner and roll the foil around it. Twist the ends to make it secure.

Horsehair and Unspun Sisal

Horsehair and unspun sisal make interesting weft materials. Arrange the fiber in a bundle of the thickness you want, and bind one end of the bundle for about a half-inch with thread of matching color.

CHAPTER 7

~~~~~~

BOARD WEAVING

The weaving frame, with its parallel, equal warp threads, produces a rectangular web; but on a board, you can weave any shape, regular or irregular, with straight or curved edges. The board serves the same purpose as the frame—a support to hold the warp while you apply the weft; but on a board, the warp threads need not be parallel—they can spread out like a fan, or like the spokes of a wheel; some can be longer than others; some can even overlap others, to form the base for a piece of three-dimensional weaving.

So, on a board, you can weave garments in sections, to be sewn together; you can weave a triangular shawl or a circular handbag; you can use the board technique for making tapestries in any shape you choose, regular or irregular.

Here are three useful board-weaving techniques.

WOODEN BOARD AND NAILS

Get a wooden board—$3/4$-inch plywood is good—somewhat bigger than the finished work will be, and some double-headed nails (they are about 3 inches long).

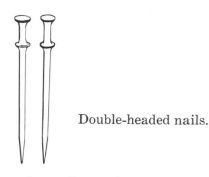

Double-headed nails.

On a sheet of paper, draw an outline of the article you want to make. Here's an important point. In this, as in all weaving techniques, the work tends to shrink as weaving progresses; with care, you can control this shrinkage, but you cannot completely eliminate it. So draw the plan 10 percent bigger in each dimension than the finished size you want. Suppose, for example, you want to weave a garment section 20 inches long by 15 inches wide; then draw it on the plan 22 inches long (20 + 10%) and 16½ inches wide (15 + 10%).

Wool is the best material for warp, because it yields to the increasing tension. Normally the warp will run the longer dimension of the work. In circular shapes, the warp threads would go across the diameter. In irregular-shaped designs, you may have considerable freedom of choice; then you would consider what arrangement would be easiest to work with, or what would best produce the desired result.

Fasten the paper that carries your pattern outline to the board with thumbtacks or tape; then drive nails around the edge of the outline to hold the warp. Space them ⅜ inch apart (for most projects, ¼ inch would be too close). Drive the nails at least ½ inch into the wood, because there will be a considerable strain on them before you have finished.

Tie one end of the warp to a corner nail, between the two heads, and stretch it from nail to nail, much as you did on the weaving frame, always placing the thread between the two heads of each nail. Tie off the other end of the warp to the last nail.

At points where the web might tend to pull in sideways, drive extra nails a few inches from the outline, and tie the selvedge to them (as you tied it to the outside of the frame).

Now prepare your weft yarn, and begin weaving in the ordinary way, except that you should not beat in so hard as you might on a frame. You will notice an advantage of the double-headed nails; they hold the warp high enough off the board that you can conveniently work with a butterfly or bodkin. Most weavers form the sheds with their fingers; but you can, if you like, try using a shed stick.

FIBERBOARD AND T-PINS

For fairly small pieces of weaving, such as a collar, in which warp tension will not be great, you can use ¾-inch fiberboard, such as is used for covering walls and ceilings. It is soft enough that you can push the T-pins into it by hand. (This is an advantage for apartment-dwellers who don't want to do a lot of hammering; and a 12- x 12-inch piece of this board makes an ideal weaving base for a bed patient.)

Draw the outline on paper and plan the warp arrangement as described above, making the same 10 percent allowance for shrinkage. Stick the T-pins in position to hold the warp threads, sloping them outward, away from the center of the work.

With this method, the warp lies flat on the surface of the board; a bodkin is convenient for passing the weft.

After the weaving is finished, the board can, for some projects, be used as an effective mounting for display purposes.

Pull out the T-pins; cover the board with burlap or linen. Then remount the finished weaving, holding it in place with some suitable short pins or nails (brass-headed finishing nails, etc.) driven in nearly flush, with just enough of the shank protruding to hold the work in place.

CARDBOARD

Cardboard makes a convenient base for weaving; it is much lighter than the board and nails, and eliminates the need for pins.

Draw your pattern directly on a piece of stiff cardboard. Cut all around, ½ *inch outside* the outline. Stick masking tape all around, to reinforce the edge. Then cut a series of slits, ½ inch apart, from the edge of the cardboard exactly to the pattern outline; these slits serve to hold the warp. The warp yarn goes through one slit, passes behind the projecting tongue of card, and out again through the next slit.

Weave in the same way as with the fiberboard and T-pins.

When the weaving is done, bend the edges of the cardboard, lift off the web, and the finished project comes free.

For a garment, use a 3-ply wool as warp, and a soft, thicker wool (handspun if available) as weft; then the weaving will proceed quickly and easily.

Circular Shapes

There are a few special technicalities in weaving circular shapes. A round shoulder bag, 10 inches in diameter, is a good project to begin with.

Warp placement on cardboard slits.

Draw the circle 10 inches in diameter and cut around ½ inch outside it. Make the cuts ½ inch apart, and you will have 67 slits. Note that, to weave in the round, you always need an odd number of warp threads. With an even number, the weft would go over and under the same warp threads every time around, and would not produce a tabby weave.

Because of the odd number of warp threads, the last one does not go right across the circle, but only from the edge to the center. To anchor it, put the end of the yarn through a small hole previously punched at the center of the circle, and tie a knot behind the card to hold it taut.

Now for the weaving.

1. Gather the warp threads together in the center; use a bodkin and a fine 2-ply wool, and start with a chain-stitch.

2. Begin weaving round and round, in tabby. It is essential to begin with a *fine* weft yarn, as recommended, because the warp threads are so closely spaced near the center. Thick weft would produce an ugly bulge. As you work farther from the center, take

care not to pull the weft too tight, or it will cause the web to buckle.

3. When you have worked about 2 inches from the center, change your weft, either by substituting a thicker wool, or by plying three lengths of the original yarn together. (This is necessary because, as you work outward, the warp threads are getting farther apart, and you need the thicker weft to fill the additional space.)

4. Weave two circles like this for the two sides of the bag, and make the strap on a frame or inkle loom, or by card weaving.

Double Weave

An interesting variant is to carry the warp right around the cardboard—through the top slits, down the back, through the bot-

Weaving a vest on a wooden board and double-headed nails. The right front half of the vest is outlined with the nails; the warp is applied on the shorter dimension; the weft is applied in tapestry technique, to create the desired pattern. Woven by Anne Robinson.

The finished vest, by Anne Robinson.

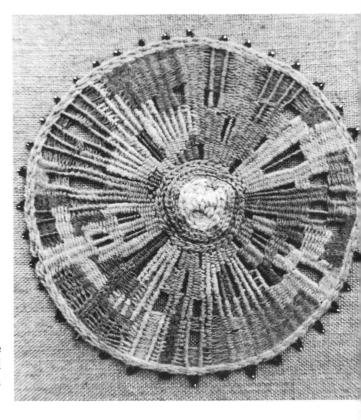

Circular wall plaque, by Christine Peters. Woven on fiberboard; mounted for display on burlap-covered wooden board.

tom slits, and up the front again, and so on. Then weave on both sides of the cardboard, carrying the weft right around the board. To allow for increasing tension, begin by packing under the warp some kind of filler—folded paper, for example—which you can pull out later as the warp tightens up.

By shaping the cardboard appropriately, you can use this method to make one-piece handbags, garments, or garment sections, etc.

Big Projects

For a fairly big piece of weaving, one layer of cardboard will probably not be stiff enough; it will bend under the warp tension. You can make a strong, yet light, base by gluing together two layers of corrugated cardboard, with the corrugations at right angles. As usual, bind the edges with adhesive tape.

Circular handbag woven on cardboard, by
Denise Fiala, with an inkle-woven shoulder
strap.

Fringed vest woven on cardboard, by Monica Fiala.

Three-dimensional tapestry on board and
nails, by Susan Fletcher.

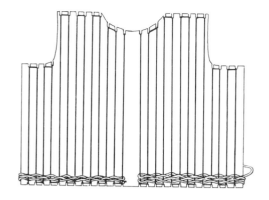

Warping plan for vest.

A Fringed Vest

This vest is a good example of garment weaving on cardboard.

1. Cut the cardboard to the shape shown, and of appropriate dimensions. Put one set of warp threads on the front, another set on the back.

2. Start weaving at the bottom, at the left of the front opening; weave tabby to the left edge of the card; carry the weft around the edge of the card, across the back, around the right edge, and to the right side of the front opening. Weave the next shot in the reverse direction.

3. Continue in this way until you reach the bottom of the armholes. From here on up, use three separate wefts, on left front, right front, and back. Continue in this way to the top.

4. The long fringe is made of separate pieces of the same warp yarn, knotted through the bottom loops of the warp.

5. Remove the vest from the board and sew the front and back sections together across the top of the shoulders.

Tree-trunk cross-section with free-form weaving on nails, by a student of the University of British Columbia School of Education.

Collar woven on cardboard, by Hilda Gerson. It utilizes tapestry and wrapped-warp techniques, and is ornamented with black bamboo beads wrapped with gold thread.

CREATIVE BOARD WEAVING

Board weaving is not the easiest of the off-loom techniques. I would certainly not advise you to try it until you have had some experience on the frame. Then you will discover that board weaving frees you from the limitations of the rectangular shape.

You can use this technique to create jewelry, using not only yarn, but beads and wire, too. By using nails of different lengths, you can have sections of the warp at different levels, for a three-dimensional effect. Instead of using plywood or cardboard, you can make the base an integral part of the project. Choose a piece of driftwood, and plan your weaving to harmonize with the lines of the grain; take a piece of tree bark, and use its indentations as part of your design.

CHAPTER 8

~~~~~~

THE SALISH FRAME

This type of frame is named after the Salish Indians of the Pacific coast, who used it to weave large blankets for domestic and ceremonial uses. On this frame, you can weave an article twice as long as the frame is high, because the warp goes right around the frame, back as well as front.

STRUCTURE

The main fixed parts of the frame are two uprights standing on a baseboard. Some weavers make their own frames. Handcraft supply stores sell them in a variety of sizes. A popular small model is 16 x 20 inches, inside measurements (i.e., 16 inches between the uprights and 20 inches vertically between the top and bottom bars). An intermediate size is 30 x 30 inches. On some of the larger models, the uprights are connected about their midpoint by a horizontal brace-board, making a structure like a capital H. On a very big frame—say, 60 x 60 inches—each upright has its own base, so that it will stand by itself while you are assembling it.

95

A notch, U-shaped or V-shaped, is cut in the top of each upright to hold the top bar. In the bottom half of each upright is bored a hole into which is fitted the bottom bar. In some models there are two or more holes, to give alternative positions for the bottom bar.

THE BARS

In the top notch, put a piece of round dowel, or a broomstick of the required length. Slide a similar stick through one pair of holes in the uprights. (For wide projects on big frames—say, more than 4 feet—some weavers find that thick bamboo makes a stiffer bar than ordinary wood.)

There's one important practical point about placement of the bottom bar. Some frames are made with only a small space between this bar and the baseboard—not enough space to pass a big ball of yarn under when you are warping the frame. So, when making or buying a frame, see that there is plenty of space between the bottom bar and the base.

You need a third stick, the floating loom-bar, around which the warp is doubled. A $\frac{1}{2}$-inch dowel, or a piece of metal curtain rod will do; it should be a little longer than the width of web you are going to make, and short enough to slide over the top and bottom bars, between the uprights. This bar is not fixed to the frame, but moves up or down as the work progresses.

This is a table-size frame. In use, to keep it steady as you work, the base could be secured to a table with a C-clamp.

WARPING THE FRAME

The Salish frame uses a continuous warp; you need not cut the warp into lengths. This feature ensures that the warp tension is self-adjusting, that is, all warp threads are at the same tension.

1. With two pieces of cord, temporarily tie the floating loom-bar to the uprights, in a horizontal position, about $\frac{3}{4}$ of the way

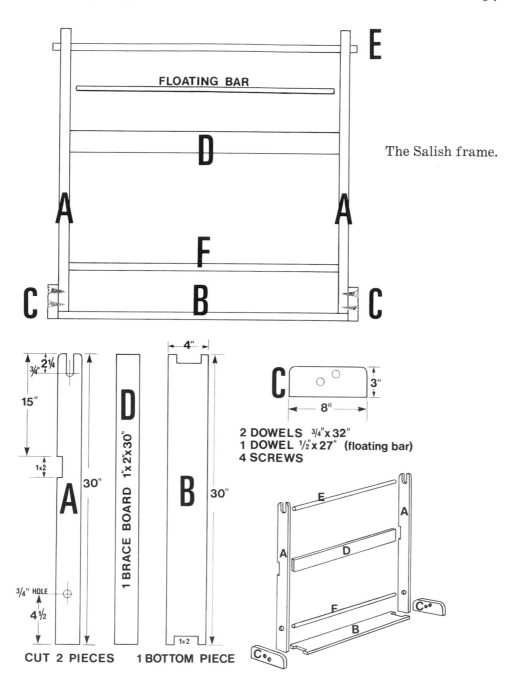

The Salish frame.

FLOATING BAR

E

D

A   A

F

C   B   C

15"

2¼
¾"

1x2

30"

A

3/4" HOLE

4½

CUT 2 PIECES

D

1 BRACE BOARD 1"x 2"x 30"

4"

B

30"

1x2

1 BOTTOM PIECE

C   3"

8"

2 DOWELS ¾"x 32"
1 DOWEL ½"x 27" (floating bar)
4 SCREWS

E

A   A

D

F

B

C   C

up the frame. (*Note*: For clarity, these cords are not shown in the diagram, and the warp is shown much more widely-spaced than it would actually be.)

2. You need to prepare for tightening of the warp as the work progresses. Put about ½ inch of packing—layers of folded paper or thin cardboard—in the upper notches, under the top bar. Alternatively, you can use wooden wedges, fully inserted at the start, and gradually withdrawn as the warp tightens.

3. You know the width of web you are going to produce; figure out where the left-hand edge of it will come on the floating loom-bar, and tie the end of the warp at that point.

4. Pass the warp over the top bar (from front to back), down the back of the frame, under the bottom bar (from back to front), up the front and over the floating loom-bar; then return in the opposite direction, under the bottom bar, up the back, over the top, down the front, and around the floating loom-bar again.

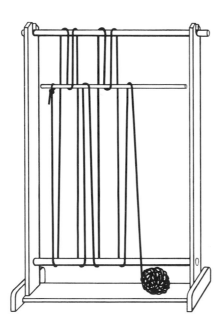

Warping the frame.

5. Continue like this till you have the required number of warp threads. (For example, a stole 15 inches wide, at 8 warp threads to the inch, would have 120 threads.) Tie the last end to the floating loom-bar.

6. Untie the floating loom-bar from the uprights; the tension of the warp now holds it in place. The traditional Indian method was to start at the top of the warp and weave downward. This was a carryover from the weighted-warp technique, where the

Partly completed weaving on the Salish frame, by Susan Hess. Twining technique. Note the packing under the top bar to control tension. The ends of the floating loom-bar can be seen, behind the finished portion of the web, about one-third of the way up from the bottom of the frame. The weaver is working from the bottom up. To create the pattern, 5 separate wefts are in use at this stage; their ends are seen hanging from the top of the web.

Wall hanging, by Kathy Robertson. Handspun wool; twining technique.

Poncho in angora wool, by Kathy Robertson.

weaver must start at the top. Some weavers like to work this way on the Salish frame, but it has no particular technical advantages.

If you decide to work downward, begin weaving immediately below the floating loom-bar and beat each row of weft upward; to work the opposite way, begin above the floating loom-bar and beat downward.

(If you want to make a fringe, *do not* begin close against the bar. Start by weaving in a strip of cardboard, of the same width as the desired length of your fringe, right across the warp. For example, for a 3-inch fringe, the card would be 3 inches wide, and as long as the warp is wide. When you start weaving with yarn, the card gives you a firm base to beat down on.)

Whichever method you choose—weaving upward or downward—move the floating loom-bar up or down to a convenient height; the warp threads slide smoothly over the top and bottom bars. Space the warp threads evenly on the floating loom-bar, and you are ready to begin.

WEAVING ON THE FRAME

Begin with a row of chaining or twining, and proceed to weave as you would on any other frame. When the level of the work gets too high for comfort (or too low, if you are working downward) simply pull the floating loom-bar down or up, and you have a fresh length of warp in position to work on.

In all work on the Salish frame, it's useful to place a sheet of cardboard between the front and back warp, so that you do not accidentally weave the two levels of the warp together.

For weaving tabby, use a shuttle and shed stick. When the warp gets too tight for efficient weaving, remove some of the packing under the top bar. (If you are working with homespun warp, it will probably stretch as you proceed. In this case, you would begin with no packing under the top bar and, when necessary, add packing so that the top bar is raised and the warp tightened.)

As you proceed, the floating loom-bar passes behind the frame, and eventually round to the front again. Finish off in the usual way with twining or chaining. There is no cutting of the warp; simply slide the floating loom-bar out to one side, and the web comes free.

There will be a row of loops remaining on each end of the web. If you have left these loops long enough, they can be cut and made into tassels or fringes. If the web is to be used as a wall hanging, you can make the top row of loops short, leave them uncut, and pass a rod through them to support the hanging.

BLANKET WEAVING

A big Salish frame can be used for weaving blankets in a variety of patterns, for use as bedspreads, couch covers, or wall hangings. For a light afghan, use tabby. For an extra-heavy blanket, do the whole web in twining.

In Chapter 4, we described how to do a single row of twining to start or finish a piece of weaving. Here are a few technical hints for weaving large areas of twining.

The two weft threads used in twining are twisted between each pair of warp threads. If you twist in the same direction on every row, the surface, after beating in, looks like a series of two-strand cords lying side by side.

But if you *reverse* the direction of the twist on alternate rows (row 1 clockwise, row 2 counterclockwise, row 3 clockwise, and so on) the finished effect is quite different; it looks like a piece of knitting. This method is sometimes called countered twining.

Countered twining requires a slightly different procedure for turning at the ends of the rows.

 Countered twining—two rows, showing end turning.

The Indians used a special variant of twining to make blankets for people of high rank. In regular twining, the double weft goes over and under one warp thread, then twists before going over and under the next. In double twining, the weft goes over and under *two* warp threads; then it is twisted and goes over and under two more. Thus, on one row, you twine the warp threads together into pairs; on the next row, you move the weave one warp thread over, so as to split those pairs.

Double twining can be woven quickly; it takes more weft yarn than single twining, but makes a very thick, luxurious-feeling blanket.

A beautiful variant is openwork twining; it is done the same as double twining, except that successive rows are spaced about an inch apart, leaving a series of openings in the web.

Openwork twining.

BLANKET DESIGNS

Traditional colors for this kind of work were white, black, and brown, although in more recent times bright colors also were used. Designs incorporated stripes, V's, diamonds, and rectangles in various combinations.

Some present-day weavers choose to follow these traditional designs, or make adaptations of them; others prefer to create entirely different designs, with little or no trace of Indian influence.

Whichever policy you adopt, you'll find that the twining method gives full freedom to your ability as a designer; the tapestry techniques described in Chapter 6 work just as well with twining as with tabby.

A hint on executing designs. There's no need to work your way right across each row in turn, making all the color changes as you go. But don't go too far in the opposite direction, and execute one whole color area first; that can lead to technical difficulties when you come to fill in narrow spaces. A safe rule is not to let any part of the pattern get more than one inch ahead of the rest; and, as in tapestry, weave decreasing shapes first.

Wall hanging, by Joyce Price; woven in tabby on open warp.

Salish blanket in traditional design of V's and crosswise stripes. Courtesy of the Museum Shop, Centennial Museum, Vancouver, British Columbia.

For complex designs, it will be helpful to have a full-size plan drawn on paper. This can be taped to the sheet of cardboard between the front and back warp, in such a position that it guides you as you work.

SADDLE BLANKET

On a Salish frame, weave a saddle blanket 40 x 32 inches. Use a heavy warp, say 8/4 cotton rug warp, 8 to the inch, and a weft of cotton or wool, the same thickness as the warp, in two or three colors.

Weave stripes near the ends of the blanket, and the main area, at the center, in one plain color, in tabby or twill weave.

TAPESTRY

The Salish frame can be used for all the techniques described in Chapter 4. It also serves very well for making large tapestries, provided you use a strong warp with good tension.

CHAPTER 9

~~~~~~

THE
WEIGHTED WARP

The weighted warp is the oldest known weaving technique. Archaeologists, excavating relics of ancient civilizations, have often found weights of stone or fired clay with center holes for tying the warp threads. Illustrations on Greek vases show the weighted warp. The technique was used in Asia Minor as early as 3000 B.C., in Europe during the Neolithic and Bronze ages, and in Palestine and in Egypt. It is still used today in Hordaland, Norway.

To suit the freer concepts of modern weaving, this ancient technique presents fantastic possibilities.

The warp threads are tied to some support at their upper ends, and are kept taut by weights at the lower ends. The top support can be an iron bar, a dowel, a piece of driftwood, a tree branch. Note that you have great freedom in the form of this top support. It need not be straight, but can be angular, curved, even a complete circular hoop if you like. Whatever its material or shape, this support should be chosen carefully, to be a natural extension of your weaving.

The bar that holds the warp must be firmly supported. You will weave more easily if this bar is free-hanging, from hooks screwed into the top of a door frame, or into the ceiling. Now you have access to both sides of the warp and you can, if you wish, weave in three dimensions.

Tie the warp threads to the bar with reversed double half-hitches, and attach the weights. In order to achieve good tension, use heavy weights such as links of a chain, big screws, metal washers, pebbles, bones, or ceramic beads.

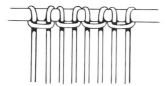

Tying warp to bar.

WEAVING WITH THE WEIGHTED WARP

Now you can begin to weave, starting at the top. Because of the variable tension, and the movement of the warp threads as they are handled, it is difficult to produce a very close, even web such as could be made on the frame. But you have great freedom in the choice of weft materials. Thick, handspun wool and heavy jute work well with the weighted warp. You can use reeds, moss, bark, etc., but with such nature materials, be sure to interweave enough yarn to hold them in position.

You will be delighted with the possibilities of the open warp. Since each warp thread is free-hanging, you can make the threads overlap, join, cross, or twist. You can use part of the warp as weft for a while, and then again as warp.

If your weights are attractive and complement the design, leave them in place after the weaving is finished. For a different effect, take off the original heavy weights and substitute lighter objects; then your weaving can be a mobile, moving with the breeze.

THE TWO-BAR METHOD

Instead of hanging a separate weight on each warp thread, you can attach a wooden bar right across the bottom of the warp. To this bottom bar, tie a loop of rope. For a big project, arrange for this loop to hang a few inches from the floor; work standing up, and put your foot into the loop to apply tension. For a medium-size project, you need not stand up; sit down, and put your leg through the loop.

The two-bar method.

WEAVING WITH STRING AND ROPE

Rope and the thicker strings are very stiff compared with wool or cotton; so to get a satisfactory weave, the warp must be very tight. You can get this tension with the two-bar method which is, in effect, a vertical adaptation of the backstrap loom.

You will enjoy working with rope and string. Jute has a dull appearance; sisal is shiny. You can use them in their natural colors, or dye them. (See Chapter 2.) Moreover, the tight-twisted, hard texture gives body and structure to the web. Adjoining wefts do not blend into each other as soft yarns will do. So by weaving with string and rope, you can create a sculptural effect with highlights and shadows, which will lead you into three-dimensional weaving.

Before you start a large project with rope, I would advise you to work first on a smaller scale—say, 18 x 24 inches—to get familiar with the handling qualities and with the decorative potential of these materials. (You may need gloves to work with rope.)

Wall hanging, by Christine Peters. Note how the pattern of the web complements the shape of the supporting stick.

Detail of wall hanging. Note how parts of the warp are used at times as weft.

Weaving on a hoop, by Gail Gretelli. Handspun wool and suede. The smaller loops are made of wrapped cane.

Weighted-warp weaving, by Rose
Naumann and Del Field, in
handspun wool.

Weighted-warp weaving, by Teresa
Pratt: handspun wool, unspun wool,
and ceramic weights. Note how the
warp is divided into sections and
brought together again.

CHAPTER 10

~~~~~~~~~~~~~~~~~~~~~~~~~~~~~~~~~~

INKLE
WEAVING

"Inkle" is an old word meaning a narrow band or strip of fabric. Ever since man began weaving, he has used such strips for bundling and carrying his belongings, as belts for clothing, and as edge-trimmings for wider fabrics. For centuries, narrow strips were woven on the bow-loom or the forked-branch loom. The modern way is to use a simple wooden frame called the inkle-loom; its small size and simplicity of operation are a delight to weavers, old and young.

A particular advantage of inkle weaving is that it goes so quickly; in just one evening, you can make two delicately patterned belts, for your own use or as gifts for friends. After a little practice, you can progress to more elaborate projects: vests, bags, skirts, cushion covers, and wall hangings.

THE INKLE-LOOM

All inkle-looms fulfill three basic requirements: a frame which holds a continuous warp; a simple method for making two sheds; a device to control warp tension.

111

The inkle-loom—store-bought or home-made—comes in two main forms. One type—sometimes called the American inkle-loom—has a strong frame on one side, and open-ended pegs; this model is especially easy to warp. The other type has frames on both sides, with crossbars between them; on this model, you can weave strips up to 12 inches wide.

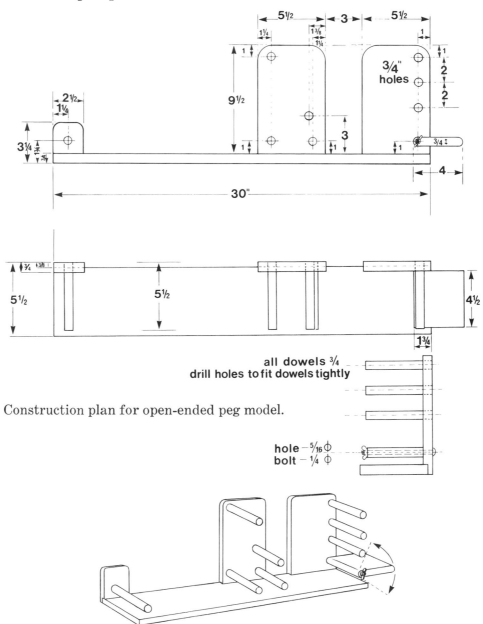

Construction plan for open-ended peg model.

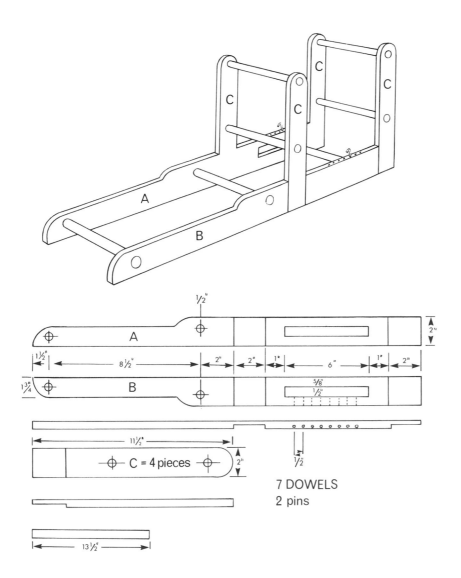

Construction plan for crossbar model.

Either type can be built for about two dollars. One hint: if you make the open-ended model, don't skimp on the dimensions of the lumber, and do take care to make all joints secure; the frame and pegs must be very strong to withstand the warp tension.

The Warp Support

Different models of loom have different number of pegs, some fixed, some movable. These serve to vary the length of the warp. On a typical frame, the minimum length is about 5 feet 6 inches. By passing the warp back and forth over the additional pegs, you can get warp to about 8 feet long.

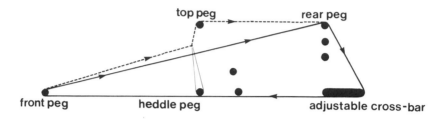

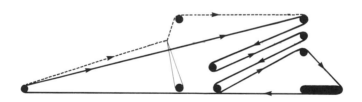

Maximum and minimum warp lengths: open-ended model; crossbar model.

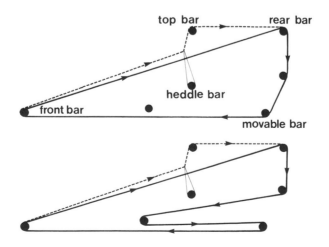

The Tension Control

The inkle process makes a warp-faced fabric in which there is considerable shortening of the warp as the work advances. The tension control device on most open-ended looms is a pivoted board, called the tension board. (Some commercially made models have a movable peg instead.) On the crossbar inkle-loom, the tension control is a movable crossbar; it usually has a range of about 6 inches, and can be fixed in various positions by metal pins slipped through holes in the frame.

Do not make or buy an inkle-loom without some kind of tension adjustment.

Making the Sheds

Weavers find that an especially enjoyable feature of the inkle-loom is the quick, easy method of making two sheds.

Refer back to the heddle bar described in Chapter 3. Loops of string (the heddles) are passed around alternate warp threads and fastened to a stick. By a pull on the heddle bar, you raise half the warp threads to form the shed.

On the inkle-loom, too, alternate warp threads pass through string heddles; the heddles are fastened to a peg. But, on the inkle-loom, the heddles, and the warp threads they hold, remain stationary; the other threads are alternately raised and lowered to form two different sheds.

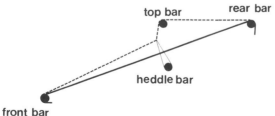

The four essential pegs.

This diagram shows the four pegs which, in much the same arrangement, form the essential working part of every inkle-loom. For clarity, only two warp threads are shown; each one represents a whole group.

One set of threads goes through the heddles, over the upper peg and then to the rear peg; this set is called the "heddle warp." The other set passes straight from the front peg to the rear peg, without going through the heddles; this is called the "open warp."

To make one shed, press with the flat of your hand on the open warp between the heddles and the rear peg; the shed opens, and you pass the weft across the web, close to the front peg. To make the opposite shed, lift the open warp with your hand in the same position.

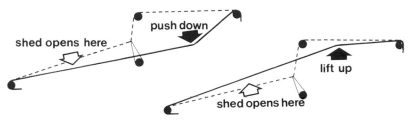

Making the two sheds.

SELECTION OF YARN

Any smooth, well-twisted yarn can be used: for example, 2-ply or 3-ply wool worsted, mercerized cotton, or smooth knitting yarns of cotton, nylon, and rayon. Smooth cotton or jute string is also suitable. The yarn should be strong, not too stretchy, and tough enough to stand the friction of shed formation.

Avoid soft, fluffy, or knobby yarns; they do not pass easily through the heddles; they cling to each other and make it hard to form a shed; they will not produce the sharp-edged patterns that are characteristic of attractive inkle bands.

For making the heddles, use a strong, thin, smooth yarn of cotton or nylon, thin twine, nylon fishline, or linen thread. The threads of the open warp will slide up and down more easily if the heddle threads are hard and smooth.

WARPING THE FRAME

Get some 2-ply or 3-ply yarn in three bright, well-contrasted colors. We'll begin with a simple pattern, to produce a series of lengthwise stripes on the band.

Warp threading patterns are drawn on two rows of squares; the top row represents the heddle warp, and the bottom row represents the open warp.

Here is the threading chart. B, W, and R represent black, white, and red yarns. (You can, of course, substitute other colors if you wish.)

Heddle warp		B	B	W	W	R	R	W	W	R	R	W	W	B	B
Open warp	B	B	W	W	R	R	W	W	R	R	W	W	B	B	

In preparation for warping, have the three colors of yarn wound in balls.

(If you do not wish to follow the chart, you can create your own arrangement of colors, and see the effect produced; but it is best not to put on too wide a warp for your first attempt.)

The threading chart is always read from left to right, putting on alternately open and heddle warp threads as indicated. The method of applying the warp is basically the same for all inkle-looms; but there are some slight differences, so we will describe each type separately.

Open-Ended Frame

1. Begin by putting on the first open warp. Tie the end of the black yarn to the front peg. (Use a knot you can easily unfasten later.)

Pass the ball of yarn straight to and over the rear peg, around the extra pegs to achieve a length of about 6 feet, over the tension device (which should be tightly screwed in the horizontal position, i.e., at greatest extension) and back to the front peg. Allowing for warp take-up and wastage, this 6-foot warp will make a nice belt.

2. Now for the first heddle warp: pass the yarn *over the top peg*, to the back peg, and right around parallel to the open warp already applied.

Lay down the ball; the friction of the yarn over the pegs will keep the warp tight enough. Now take the yarn that is to make your heddles; loop it around the heddle peg, over the warp thread you have just put on, and back down to the heddle peg. Tighten the heddle loop, pulling on the warp thread until it lies exactly beside the open warp thread that was previously put on. Cut the heddle yarn and tie it.

3. Make 13 more heddle loops the same length as the first, for use on the other threads of the heddle warp. (We cannot give

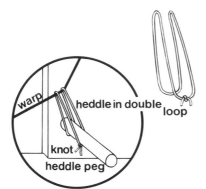

Heddle for open-ended frame.

specific instructions that the heddle loops should be so many inches long, because different home-made or store-bought frames differ somewhat in their dimensions. You have to determine the length of the first one by experiment, and then make the others the same.)

To apply each heddle, fold the loop in half, put its center over the warp thread, and slide the two ends of the loop over the heddle peg; keep the knot underneath the peg.

4. Apply 2 more black threads, one open and one through a heddle. Cut the black yarn where it passes over the front peg. Untie the knot holding the other end of the yarn to the front peg, and tie the two ends together with a knot close against the front peg. Don't worry about the fact that these two threads cross over the others at the front peg. That does not matter, because this

short section of warp will not be woven, anyway. Note that this entire black portion of the warp—2 threads open and 2 through heddles—is now one continuous thread, not tied to any peg, and free to slide around the frame, over the pegs.

5. Tie the end of the white yarn to the front peg and apply 4 white warp threads, 2 open and 2 through heddles. Similarly cut the white yarn at the front peg; untie the knot holding the other end and tie the two ends together.

6. Continue like this. Apply in turn 4 red threads, 4 white, 4 red, 4 white, and the last 4 black. Cut the yarn when each color group is complete and tie its two ends together.

Crossbar Frame

Lay the frame on its side; then you can easily pass the ball of yarn around the pegs.

Apply the first 2 black warp threads as described for the open-ended frame. Find the correct length for the first heddle. With this frame, you obviously cannot slide heddle loops over the end of the heddle bar, so the heddle is put over the warp thread, and fastened to the bar with a snitch knot.

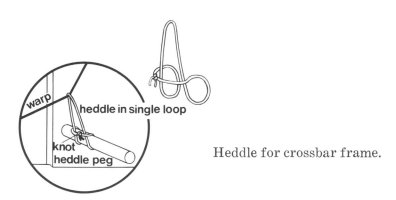

Heddle for crossbar frame.

Here, too once you have found the correct length for the first heddle, cut 13 more to the same length; tie them all to the bar, in the same way as the first one.

Now, when you apply each heddle warp thread, simply put the ball of yarn through the heddle loop before passing it over the top bar. (Obviously, the ball of yarn must not be too big, or it won't go through the heddle loop.)

Apart from this slight difference, the warp is applied in the same way as on the open-ended frame. Arrange it so that the completed warp is roughly centered on the crossbars.

WEAVING THE INKLE

Sit at the loom, with the front peg nearest to you. With the open-ended type, you can rest one end of the baseboard on your lap, the other end on a table or on the floor.

For weft, use the same black yarn that forms the selvedge of your warp; then the turnovers of weft at the selvedges will be inconspicuous. You can form the weft into a butterfly, wind it into a small ball, or wind it on one of the shuttles used for other kinds of weaving.

Before you begin, make sure that the warp threads are lying close together. From the front peg to the heddles, they should be touching, with not the slightest gap between them.

With this close-packed warp, you cannot use a fork or comb for beating in, so you will need a thin, flat stick; slide it horizontally into the shed and beat toward the front peg. Some weavers prefer to use the edge of the hand; or, if you are using the Norwegian shuttle, you can beat in with its straight edge.

Now to begin. With one hand, depress the open warp between the heddles and the rear peg; a shed opens between the heddles and the front peg. If the shed does not open clear, put one or two fingers into the shed, near the heddles, and pull toward you, opening the shed wide, right down as close as it will go to the front peg. Pass the first shot of weft from right to left, leaving 2 inches hanging on the right.

(Alternatively, if you want to leave some unwoven warp for a fringe, insert a 4- or 5-inch strip of card into the first shed; then make another shed and pass the first shot of weft as described above.)

Now raise the open warp between the heddles and the rear

Inkle-weaving patterns.

Band No. 1 illustrates four of the techniques described in the text. *Left to right,* dot or dash; thin line; variable line; stripe; variable line; thin line; dot or dash.

Band No. 2. A "ladder" pattern, produced from the following warp arrangement, using a black weft.

Heddle warp	B	B	W	W	W	W	B	B	B	W	W	B	B	B	W	W	W	W	B	B	B
Open warp	B	B	W	W	B	B	W	W	W	W	W	W	B	B	B	B	W	W	B	B	B

Band No. 3. A broad central white stripe with a modified checkerboard section on each side. Warp arrangement in black, red, green, and white; with black weft.

Heddle warp	B	R	R	R	B	G	G	G	B	R	R	R	B	W	W	W	W	B	R	R	R	B	G	G	G	B	R	R	R	B	B
Open warp	B	G	G	G	B	R	R	R	B	G	G	G	B	W	W	W	W	B	G	G	G	B	R	R	R	B	G	G	G	B	B

Band No. 4. The "flower" pattern is worked on the right-hand side of this band in a light-colored yarn against the dark background.

Band No. 5 shows the split-band technique. At the end of each split-band section, the weft is pulled quite tight, to bunch the warp together. About 1 inch of warp is left unwoven before the next split-band section is begun.

Bands Nos. 6 and 7 show various pickup techniques on two-color crossbar patterns.

Vest, by Peggy Turner, made of 16 inkle bands sewn together.

peg. A new shed opens. First put that loose end of weft through from right to left, then pass the butterfly or shuttle through from left to right. Beat in, change the shed, and keep passing the weft in the usual way, back and forth. Now the weft is firmly anchored at this end, and will not come loose later when the band is taken off the frame. (Any projecting end of weft can be trimmed off.)

Weft Tension

Correct tension of the weft helps to produce a neat-looking band. Pull each weft tight enough to make the warp threads lie snugly together, with no sight of the weft between them. There should be no loose weft at the selvedges, only a neat, close, U-turn of weft yarn over the outside warp threads.

Variations of weft tension will alter the width of the band. To be sure of maintaining uniform width, keep a ruler handy and check frequently. (A short ruler makes a good beater and lets you kill two birds with one stone.)

Beating In

Beat in firmly, so that successive weft threads are pressed fairly close together. Take care to beat *uniformly*, with the same pressure on every shot: otherwise, when you come to weave more complex patterns, some pattern units—bars, checkers, etc.—will be stretched out, and others will be compressed.

You can check this point by watching the length of each pattern unit as it is formed.

Joining Weft

When the weft in your butterfly or shuttle is nearly used up, start a new length by passing the new and old weft threads together for two shots. Beat these rows in hard, so that the extra weft thickness does not disrupt the pattern.

Weaving a necktie on open-ended frame. This shows the method of reducing width by cutting out warp threads, two at a time. The Norwegian shuttle is in position for beating in.

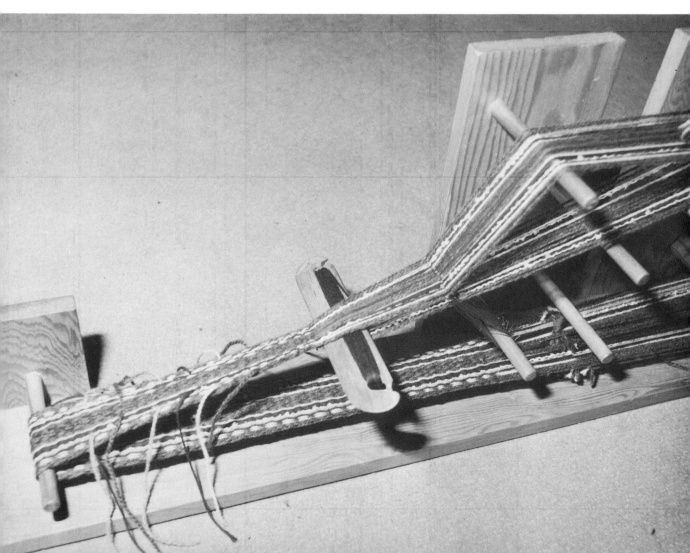

Moving the Band

When you have worked fairly close to the heddles, you find the sheds becoming so narrow that you can't conveniently pass the weft.

1. Slack off the tensioning device.

2. Pull the band toward you, so that the woven part slides around and under the front peg. You may have to move it a few inches at a time, pausing to slide the heddles back along the warp. You may need to pull on the warp elsewhere along its length, to help it slip over some of the pegs. With the open frame, and a wide inkle, take care that some of the warp threads do not slip off the ends of the pegs. (You can twist an elastic band several times around the open end of each peg to form a kind of rim or lip that helps to prevent warp threads from slipping off.)

3. Continue moving the band till the last completed row is about an inch from the front peg. Readjust the tension control to tighten the warp, and begin weaving again from the front peg toward the heddles.

Warp Tension

As the warp tightens up during weaving, release the tension control, bit by bit, to compensate. Try to keep the tension as near constant as possible throughout; this helps to keep the pattern uniformly proportioned all along the band.

Finishing Off

When the tied ends of the warp have moved right around between the rear peg and the upper peg, you find it becomes difficult to make a shed. Proceed as follows.

1. Weave as far as you can then, after the last shot, cut the weft, leaving about 6 inches hanging.

2. Cut the heddle warp close to the upper peg, and the open

warp right below the upper peg. (Don't cut the heddles; you can use them again.)

3. Remove the band from the frame. Take the loose end of weft, and the two outside warp threads on the same side; tie them all together with an overhand knot. Also knot the two outside warp threads on the other edge of the band. There is no risk now of the end unraveling. Trim all warp ends to an even length.

4. The loose warp ends can be made into fringes, braids, or tassels (see Chapter 12); or, if you want a buckle-fastening, cut off the warp ends, sew the buckle to one end of the inkle, and overcast or machine-stitch the other end to keep it firm.

PLANNING AN INKLE PATTERN

Here are some of the basic warp arrangements that may be used to make up inkle patterns. (The examples mention black and white: the same principles, of course, apply to any contrasting colors.)

The Dot or Dash

Heddle warp	B		W		B
Open warp		B		B	

A single white thread set among several black ones produces a row of dots or dashes running lengthwise down the band.

Thin Line

Heddle warp	B		W		B	
Open warp		B		W		B

Two adjoining white threads produce a thin white line on a black background.

Variable Line

Heddle warp		B		W		W		B	
Open warp	B		B		W		B		B

Three adjoining white threads produce a line that is alternately 1 thread and 2 threads wide.

Stripe

Heddle warp		B	W		W		B	B	
Open warp	B		B	W		W		B	B

Four adjoining white threads produce a continuous stripe 2 threads wide. To make wider stripes, increase the number of adjoining threads of the same color—5, 6, etc.

Bars

Heddle warp		W	W	W	W
Open warp	B	B	B	B	

A group of white threads on the heddle warp and black on the open warp (or vice versa) will produce a series of crosswise bars.

Checkers

Heddle warp	W	W	W	W	B	B	B	B	W	W	W	W
Open warp		B	B	B	B	W	W	W	W	B	B	B

The checkerboard consists of a series of short bars in alternating colors on the heddle warp and open warp.

Flower

Heddle warp		D		D		D		L		L		D		D		D	
Open warp	D		D		D		L		D		L		D		D		D

The "flower" effect depends on using different yarn thicknesses as well as different colors. This pattern makes a narrow, two-color belt. For the dark color (D) use a fine 2-ply or 3-ply yarn; for the light color (L) use a heavy 5-ply yarn. Use the dark color for weft; take care to beat in evenly, so the pattern is uniform. The light "flowers" will stand out above the dark background.

A Bar-Pattern Band

Here is the threading chart for a band with a dark-colored border and a center section of dark and light bars.

Heddle warp		D		D		L		L		L		L		L		L		L		L		L		D		D	
Open warp	D		D		D		D		D		D		D		D		D		D		D		D		D		D

Use a D-colored weft.

A Three-Color Checkerboard

This pattern gives a checkerboard of two colors inside a border of a third.

Heddle warp		X		X		#		#		#		#		O		O		O		O		#		#		#		#		X		X	
Open warp	X		X		O		O		O		O		#		#		#		#		O		O		O		O		X		X

You can make some variations on this pattern. The basic

checkerboard effect is obtained by beating just hard enough to form a series of perfect squares down the center of the band. Heavy beating will flatten the checkers into a series of bicolored crosswise bars.

For a four-color effect, replace the four #-color threads in the open warp with another color.

THE PICKUP TECHNIQUE

Plain inkle weaving produces a uniform pattern right along the band. Here is a popular way to vary the pattern. The pickup technique works best on a crossbar pattern. Try this one in black and white.

Heddle warp		B		B	W	W	W	W	W	W	W	W	W	W	B	B
Open warp	B	B	B	B	B	B	B	B	B	B	B	B	B	B	B

Set up the warp and weave several shots with B weft to make a section of the plain bar pattern.

The basic operation of this method is to raise black threads from the open warp so that they form part of what would otherwise be the plain white bars. By picking up these black threads in proper order, you can make diagonals, chevrons, diamonds, checkerboards, and so on. Here is the way to make a diagonal.

1. Make a down shed (i.e., by pressing down on the open warp), but before you pass the weft, reach down through the heddle warp and pull up the 3rd black thread from the left in the open warp. (Some weavers use their fingers for picking up threads; others use a knitting needle.) Pass the weft.

This extra black thread is called a "float thread" because it remains on top of the band for one extra shed instead of going below with the rest of the open warp.

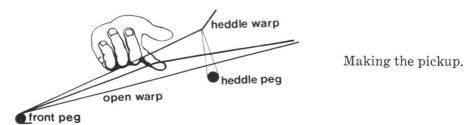

Making the pickup.

2. Make an up shed (i.e., by raising the open warp) and pass weft in the ordinary way.

3. On the next down shed, pick up the 4th black thread from the left. Pass the weft.

4. Make an ordinary up shed and pass weft.

5. Pick up the 5th black thread, then the 6th, and so on, until you have worked the diagonal across to the right border. Then work back from right to left, for a diagonal sloping the other way.

More Hints on Pickup

You can pick up two or more threads at once. For example, to make a chevron, first pick up the 8th black thread. On the next down shed, pick up Nos. 7 and 9; on the next, Nos. 6 and 10, and so on, till the two diagonals reach the borders. Reverse the process to turn the chevron into a diamond.

The more threads there are in the pattern area of the band (i.e., the two-color part between the borders), the more variety of pattern you can get. The belt shown on page 121 (No. 6) has 16 black and 17 white threads between the borders. Study this belt carefully, then experiment and use your imagination.

One warning: don't float the same thread twice running. Overlong float threads will get snagged when the band is taken off the frame and put to use.

PROMINENT PICKUP PATTERNS

The methods described above produce fairly thin pattern outlines, consisting of single warp threads. You can also make more prominent patterns, with lines that are wider, or raised above the surface of the band. Try these techniques.

1. Instead of picking up one thread at a time from the open warp, pick up two adjoining threads. This will give you pattern outlines twice as wide as those produced by picking up one thread. This method is specially suitable for use where you want only part of a pattern to be prominent; elsewhere on the band, you can continue picking up one thread at a time to make thinner lines.

2. This method makes thick pattern lines all over the band. When warping the frame, use a thicker yarn for the open warp than for the heddle warp. If this method were applied to the threading chart given above, the black threads picked up from the open warp would make wide pattern lines, raised above the surface of the band.

3. We have so far given threading charts that place alternate warp threads through the heddles; but for prominent pickup patterns you can use *two* open warp threads between each pair of heddles, in the pattern-part of the band. For example:

Heddle warp		B	B		W		W		W		W		W		W		W		W		B		B
Open warp	B		B	BB		BB		BB		BB		BB		BB		BB		BB	B		I

At each pickup, raise the double thread. For even heavier pattern lines, use this double warp method with a thick yarn.

There's one point to watch with this technique. You may be floating two sets of two warp threads at one shot (e.g., in making a diamond pattern); then less than 90 percent of the warp remains in the shed. So control weft tension with special care, to avoid making the band too narrow at this point.

SPLIT BAND

An interesting variation is to split the band in two for some distance, then rejoin it.

1. Put in an extra weft and, to anchor it, weave two shots with both wefts at once.

2. Begin weaving halfway across with each weft. The band splits in two.

3. When the slit is long enough, weave straight across the warp with both wefts to close the slit. After two shots, cut one weft and continue weaving normally with the other.

Make the slit near one end of a belt; to fasten the belt around your waist, put the other end of the band through the slit, and pull tight.

DIFFERENT MATERIALS

Modern weavers are experimenting with unconventional materials for inkle weaving. The following notes will give you some ideas on what to try. But remember to use thick or rough materials in the open warp only. For the heddle warp, which must slip through the heddles, use only the smooth, hard-twisted yarns described earlier.

Leather. Narrow strips of suede or other varieties of leather, in various textures and colors.

Wool. Handspun wool can be used, so long as it is fairly tight-spun. Very soft, fluffy wool would create difficulties, even in the open warp.

Jute. String of various colors, thicknesses, and textures.

Beads. Thread small beads on one or more threads of the open warp as you are warping the frame. They will later be spaced at regular intervals as the band is woven. Put on plenty of beads at the start; push them ahead as you work. To put one bead in place, slide it down the thread, close to the completed part of the band; pass the weft ahead of it, and it is locked in place. Any surplus beads can be removed when you cut the warp to take the finished band off the frame.

SHORT INKLE BANDS

For some purposes you may want inkle bands considerably shorter than the minimum length your frame will handle. Suppose you want a band 24 inches long and your frame, at its shortest adjustment, takes a 5-foot warp.

Weave the 24-inch band. Leave a few inches of warp unwoven, then begin weaving again and use the rest of the warp to make another 24-inch band, matching the first, if you like, or different from it. In this way you utilize the spare length of warp.

Cut at the unwoven section to separate the two bands.

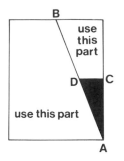

Cutting bamboo placemat.

A PARTY TWIRL

To make this party decoration, take a matchstick bamboo place-mat and cut it as shown.

B is the midpoint of the top end. Cutting in this way gives pieces of graduated length, from the full width of the mat down to CD. The pieces in the shaded area, ACD, are too short to use.

One mat gives enough bamboo for four twirls. For an open-ended frame, it does not matter how wide the mat is. For the crossbar frame, discard any pieces that are longer than the length of the crossbars.

1. Set up a warp that will give a brightly colored inkle, suited to any other decorations you have. Plan your own pattern, with about 36 threads, or use the four-color checkerboard pattern on page 128, extended to 36 threads by two more border threads on each side. For warp and weft use 8-cord cable twist crochet cotton. (Don't substitute a different yarn, or the finished band will not twirl properly.) The band should be about 1 inch wide. On the crossbar frame, put the warp far over on the left side of the bars.

2. Weave in the ordinary way for about 2 inches; then, instead of passing weft, insert the shortest bamboo stick into the shed. Change shed, beat in, and pass weft.

3. Take a bamboo stick a bit longer than the first one, and put it in the next shed. Change shed and pass another shot of weft.

4. Continue like this, alternating bamboo sticks—each one a little longer than the one before—and shots of weft. Beat in as strongly as you can.

5. When you have inserted the longest stick, weave 2 more inches ordinary tabby. Take the warp off the loom. You now have a shape like this.

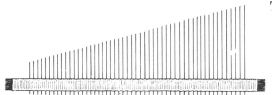 Twirl as removed from inkle-loom.

6. Slide alternate sticks through the band so that they project to the left instead of to the right. You now have a symmetrical triangular shape.

7. Braid or tie the unwoven warp at the top into a loop to hang from the ceiling. Make the warp ends at the bottom into a tassel. Tie a pine cone, bell, or other ornament weighing a few ounces to the bottom of the band.

8. Hang the band up. Give it a good twist, and it will stay twisted. Decorate the ends of the bamboo sticks with tinsel, tiny glass balls, etc.

Ski cap. An inkle band forms the brim and tassel of the cap. The crown is woven on a circle of cardboard. (*Photo: Jack Buquet*)

Cushion cover by Karen Brummel in natural-color gray and black wool: inkle-woven bands and tapestry panels.

Wall hanging with pockets, by Geri McPhee, made of inkle bands and card-woven bands sewn together. (*Ulli Steltzer*)

GUITAR STRAPS

Inkle bands make beautiful guitar straps; but wool has an affinity for static electricity, and tiny wool fibers would in time get into the mechanism of an electric guitar and ruin the instrument.

So for this purpose, always use mercerized cotton warp and weft. Using the split-band technique described above, make three buttonholes near one end of the strap for easy adjustment of length.

WEAVING NECKTIES

The main technical difference between a necktie and any other inkle band is that it is much wider at one end than at the other. Here's how to make it.

1. Measure a store-bought necktie to find the proper dimensions. Set up your warp the full width of the wide end, and begin weaving as usual.

2. To make the band narrower, begin cutting out warp threads, two at a time, from matching parts of the pattern, one on each side of center. Cut the warp threads 2 inches ahead of the last shot of weft, and later darn the ends back into the completed portion.

3. Continue cutting threads two at a time, gradually tapering the tie till it is narrow enough for the part that goes around the neck. When weaving this part, pull the weft very tight.

4. When the neck portion is finished, slack off the weft a little; this will make the other end of the tie somewhat wider.

5. Hemstitch or machine-stitch across both ends of the tie, then cut off the loose warp ends.

RUG WEAVING ON THE INKLE-LOOM

You can use the crossbar type of inkle-loom for making large knotted rugs; weave a number of strips of rug the full width of the loom (12 inches on the large size) and sew them together to make a rug of the width you want.

Be sure that the tension device is well extended when you start. Not only must it accommodate the shortening of the warp; you will have to slacken it off still more to let the thick, pile-covered portion of the strip pass over the crossbars.

CHAPTER 11

~~~~~~~~~~~~~~~~~~~~~~~~~~~~~~~~

CARD WEAVING

Card or tablet weaving is one of the most ancient textile processes, and was traditionally used to make belts or narrow bands of fabrics in complex patterns. Tablet weaving had reached a high state of development in Egypt four thousand years ago, its technical secrets safeguarded by a guild of belt-weavers. From Egypt, the method spread to North Africa, Japan, China, northern Europe, and Iceland. About the beginning of the Christian era, card weaving was being combined with loom weaving to produce a piece of ordinary cloth with a card-woven border.

In each country, the method was used for different purposes, and with different materials. In China and Japan, for example, silk was much used; card weavers of Persia and Caucasia combined silk with threads of gold and silver.

Card weaving takes its name from the pieces of card, punched with holes, through which the warp is threaded. Tablet weaving—an older name for the technique—refers to the perforated tablets of fired clay, tortoise shell, or leather that were formerly used.

Card weaving makes a warp-faced fabric; the weft is unseen

except for small loops at the edges. The threads carried by each card (usually 4 per card) become twisted together into one thicker thread; this gives great lengthwise strength to the finished band. (Card-woven bands have been used for pack-straps, camel harnesses, and other such heavy-duty functions.)

The pattern is obtained by use of different-colored warp threads, and by turning the cards in a given sequence to repeat or vary the design. As far as appearance goes, both sides of a card-woven band look good, though they never show exactly the same pattern.

These traditional techniques for producing elaborately patterned bands are still of interest to many weavers; but card weaving today offers a new challenge—using large numbers of cards to produce wider fabrics, and manipulating warp bundles to create designs, or to weave in three dimensions.

THE CARDS

The most popular shape is the square, with four holes.

You can buy ready-made cards, of cardboard or plastic; or you can make them from smooth, stiff cardboard to the dimensions indicated. Make 20 for a start. Cut the cards, round off the corners, and punch the holes. Mark the holes with letters as shown, and number the cards from 1 to 20.

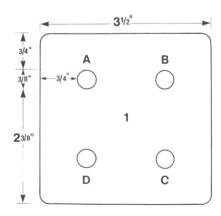

Square card, showing dimensions.

Card-weaving patterns. No. 1. Belt with lengthwise stripe: blue, yellow, red, and green warp; blue weft; continuous forward turning.

	↗	↗	↗	↗	↘	↘	↘	↘
A	B	Y	R	G	G	R	Y	B
B	B	Y	R	G	G	R	Y	B
C	B	Y	R	G	G	R	Y	B
D	B	Y	R	G	G	R	Y	B
	1	2	3	4	5	6	7	8

The pattern could be adapted for more cards and more colors.
No. 2. Belt with crosswise bars: red, yellow, and blue warp; red weft; continuous forward turning.

	↗	↗	↗	↗	↘	↘	↘	↘
A	R	Y	Y	Y	Y	Y	Y	R
B	R	Y	Y	Y	Y	Y	Y	R
C	R	B	B	B	B	B	B	R
D	R	B	B	B	B	B	B	R
	1	2	3	4	5	6	7	8

The pattern could be adapted for more cards, or for thinner crossbars.
No. 3. Braided belt, woven from chart and instructions on page 148.
Nos. 4 & 5. Two sections of one belt woven from the threading chart on page 139 in red, white and blue, illustrating how one threading can produce different patterns. No. 4 shows diamond and crossbar, formed by starting from CD position (D nearer the weaver), 4 quarter-turns forward, 4 back. No. 5 shows St. Andrew's crosses formed by starting from AB position (B nearer the weaver), 4 quarter-turns forward, 4 back.
No. 6. Belt from the following pattern, supplied by Denise Fiala: blue, green, yellow, and red warp; blue weft.

	↗	↘	↗	↗	↗	↗	↗	↗	↗	↗	↗	↘	↘	↘	↘	↘	↘	↘	↘	↗	↘
A	B	G	B	B	B	Y	Y	R	R	Y	G	Y	R	R	Y	Y	B	B	B	G	B
B	B	G	B	B	Y	Y	R	R	Y	G	B	G	Y	R	R	Y	Y	B	B	G	B
C	B	G	B	Y	Y	R	R	Y	G	B	B	B	G	Y	R	R	Y	Y	B	G	B
D	B	G	Y	Y	R	R	Y	G	B	B	B	B	G	Y	R	R	Y	Y	G	B	
	1	2	3	4	5	6	7	8	9	10	11	12	13	14	15	16	17	18	19	20	21

Turn 12 quarter-turns forward, 12 quarter-turns back, to form the pattern sequence: diamond, chevron, X, chevron, diamond, and so on.

YARNS FOR CARD WEAVING

For card weaving, choose yarns firm in texture and nonfuzzy on the surface. They need not be absolutely smooth-surfaced (cotton chenille, for example, has been successfully used), but there should be no loose fibers. On some soft wool yarns, for example, the loose fibers eventually form tangles of fluff that hinder the movement of the warp through the holes in the cards; or pieces of fluff get incorporated into the web and spoil the clean-cut lines of the pattern.

Tightly twisted cotton, linen, silk, wool, and jute yarns, wool and cotton rug yarn, and many of the synthetic yarns are good for card weaving. Caution: do not at first mix different yarns in one project—wool and synthetics, for example—for if one stretches and the other does not, you cannot get an evenly woven band.

Use strong, contrasting colors. The weft is usually the same color as the warp threads on the two outside cards, so that the end loops of the weft are not conspicuous on the selvedges.

In figuring quantities of yarn, allow for wastage at the ends, and for the take-up in length caused by the repeated twistings of the warp. To be on the safe side, make the warp 24 inches longer than the finished band you require.

MAKING A BELT

Here is the threading chart for a belt with a diamond pattern. Use for warp some yarn that is just slightly stretchy: this makes it easier to maintain correct tension as you work. I would suggest, too, that you choose a medium-thick yarn for this first effort—it will not take long to finish.

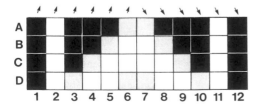

Threading chart for belt.

Each vertical column of the chart represents one card; the 12 columns, numbered left to right, show that this pattern requires 12 cards.

The four squares in each column, marked A, B, C, and D, represent the four holes in each card. The black, white, or gray color of each square indicates which of the three colors is to be threaded in that hole. (You do not have to use black, white, or gray—choose three well-contrasted colors to suit your own taste.)

The sloping arrows at the top of the chart indicate which way the cards are to be threaded. To remember which symbol means what, think of it this way.

You always hold the card face up for threading, to see the letters beside the holes.

The upward-pointing arrow means that you thread the yarn through the holes *upward*—that is, from back to front of the card. Tie the four ends together in front of the card.

The downward-pointing arrow means that you thread the yarn through the holes *downward*—that is, from front to back of the card. Tie the four ends together behind the card.

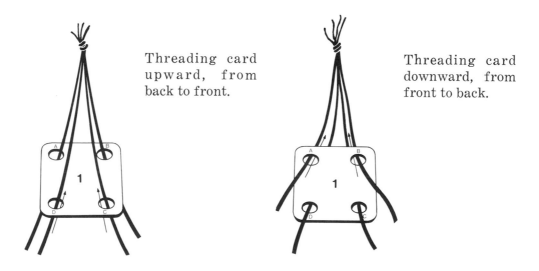

Threading card upward, from back to front.

Threading card downward, from front to back.

(Note that all threads in one card *must* enter the holes the same way, or, when you try to weave, the card will not turn.)

All threading charts are drawn in much the same way as this; the only difference is in the symbols used to indicate the various colors—initial letters of the colors, typographical signs such as #, *, etc.

Now let's begin.

1. Cut the warp. See how many threads you need of each color. In this instance it is:

$$\begin{array}{l} 20 \text{ black} \\ 18 \text{ white} \\ \underline{10 \text{ gray}} \\ 48 = 12 \text{ cards, four threads each} \end{array}$$

Cut the threads 6 feet long.

2. Thread the first card as shown in the chart with 4 black threads, passed through upward, from back to front. Pull about 8 inches of each thread through the holes, then tie the four ends together in front of the card. Lay the card face down on the table, with the four loose ends stretched out straight. Similarly thread cards 2 to 6, with the proper color in each hole; tie the four threads of each card together; lay face down on top of card No. 1, with the A, B, C, and D holes all in the same positions, one on top of another.

Thread card 7 downward, from front to back. Pull about 8 inches of each thread through the holes, then tie the four ends together behind the card. Lay it face down on the pile. Similarly thread cards 8 to 12. (You will save yourself some labor if you carefully keep all the loose ends of warp parallel, and without tangles.)

3. Put an elastic band over the knotted ends of the warp, slide it along and snap it around the bundle of cards, to keep them in order.

4. Tie the knotted ends of the warp together with a strong cord. Comb through the warp with your fingers to get the threads parallel. Gather the loose ends into two equal-sized bundles and tie the bundles together with two overhand knots (a reef knot). Tie another strong cord to this end of the warp and fasten it to something solid—a doorknob, a C-clamp on a table, etc.

The other end of the warp (i.e., where the cards are) is tied to a chair-back; weight the chair, if necessary, to maintain tension. Sit on another chair beside the warp as you weave.

If you must often put away your work and bring it out again, a convenient method is to stretch the warp around the pegs of an inkle-loom. Place the cards in the normal working space of the loom, between the front and upper pegs. Move the completed band toward yourself as the work advances. Handled like this, the warp remains always in order, at correct tension, ready for work at a moment's notice.

Weaving the Belt

Remove the elastic band from the bundle of cards, and slide it along the warp, out of the way. Check that all cards are facing the same way, printed side toward your left, and that all are in what we call the AD position—holes A and D on top, and A nearer to the end at which you are going to begin work.

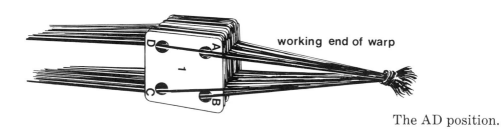

working end of warp

The AD position.

Slide the cards back and forth a few inches on the warp; this will open up the shed. Let the cards come to rest about 6 inches from the end.

Now, in the first inch or two, close to the knots, the warp threads are bunched together; so before beginning the actual weaving, you must spread them to the proper width.

Take a piece of coarse, stiff cord and make one shot with it as if it were weft. Give the cards a quarter-turn toward you, slide them back and forth to open the shed, and insert another shot of the cord. Turn the cards back to AD position; make another shot. Give a quarter-turn forward; make another shot. Return to AD position—another shot. Repeat the process till all warp threads are lying smooth, parallel, and just touching.

For weft, use the same yarn as that in cards 1 and 12. Make some of this into a butterfly, or wind it on a shuttle. With the cards in AD position, pass one shot. Leave about 3 inches of weft hanging out.

Give the cards a quarter-turn forward, away from you, so that D goes down; A and B are now on top, B toward you. Slide the cards back and forth to open the shed. First put the loose end of weft through this shed to anchor it; then pass the shuttle or butterfly.

The warp in card weaving is so closely packed that you can't beat in with a comb or fork; so put the edge of your hand into the shed and push the weft firmly down; or if you are using the Norwegian shuttle, beat in with the straight, narrow edge of it.

Give two more quarter-turns in the same direction till the cards are once again in the AD position. Then give four quarter-turns in the reverse direction, back again to the AD position, passing one shot of weft after each quarter-turn.

Some Practical Hints

1. Maintain an even tension on the weft; if it becomes slack, the warp threads sag apart, the band becomes wider, and the pattern becomes disjointed. If you pull the weft too tight, the band gets narrower.

2. See that each shed is cleanly made, with all warp threads raised and lowered as they should be. If one thread is stuck in the wrong position, move it with your fingers. It also helps, if some threads are sticking, to separate the cards a little, from side to side, and move them back and forth on the warp.

3. Card weaving needs concentration. If you are trying to weave and talk or listen to the radio at the same time, it's easy to forget whether you are turning forward or backward. (And if you resume turning in the wrong direction, the pattern will be different.)

4. If you want to stop work part-way through, get the cards

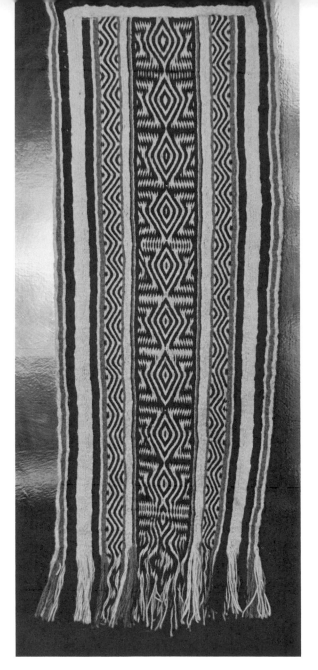

Wide-card weaving, by Madelaine Chisholm.

in "home position," AD, at the completion of one cycle of four-forward-four-reverse turns. Slide the elastic band back to the cards, to hold them till you begin again.

Finishing the Belt

Continue till you have not enough warp for one more complete pattern. Stop with the cards in home position. Tie the end of the weft to one of the outside warp threads.

Remove the belt from its supports, untie the knots at the ends of the warp, slide off the cards, and pull out the few shots of cord you used as temporary weft at the start.

To finish the ends:

1. Make the unwoven warp ends into fringes, by one of the methods described in Chapter 12.

2. For square ends, machine-stitch or overcast-stitch across the ends to hold the warp and the last few shots of weft together. Cut off surplus warp ends.

3. To apply a buckle, square off both ends and sew the buckle on one end. Alternatively you can use a tongued buckle on one end and sew to the other end a leather strap pierced with holes.

VARIATIONS

In card weaving, you can produce many different patterns from one threading of the cards. This variety is a source of keen interest and pleasure to many card weavers—even those with long experience.

To demonstrate some of the variety attainable, thread your cards to the same chart you used before (with the same colors, or different ones if you like). Try some of the techniques described below; you will produce a belt very different from the first one.

Multiple Forward Turns

Begin at the home position, AD, and make 4 quarter-turns forward, passing a shot of weft each time. Then, instead of reversing the movement, continue making quarter-turns forward, with a shot of weft after each one. This produces a pattern of large chevrons, extending nearly to the edges of the band.

You can, if you wish, continue like this right to the end. If you do, you will find, after five or six turns, that the unwoven section of the warp is so tightly twisted that you have difficulty moving the cards. The remedy:

1. Pause with the cards in home position and fasten them with the elastic band.

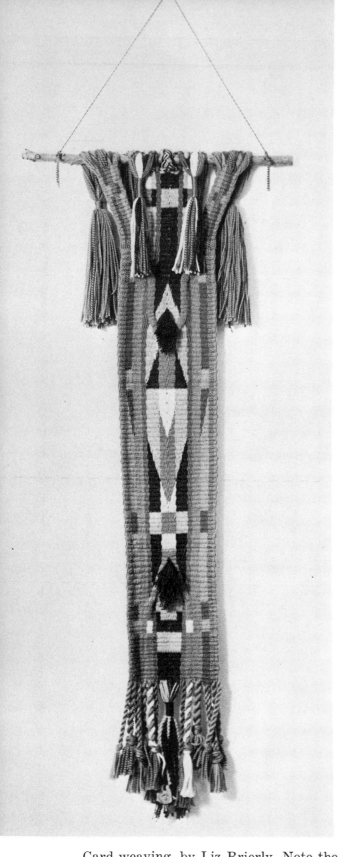

Card weaving, by Liz Brierly. Note the interesting tassels and twisted fringe on this piece.

Detail of card weaving, by Byron Johnstad.

2. Untie the unwoven end of the warp and get the threads straight and parallel again. Retie, and resume weaving.

3. Repeat the straightening as often as may be necessary.

Because of the trouble involved in straightening the warp, this is not the most popular card-weaving technique.

You can avoid that extra trouble by the following modification.

Do a *limited number*—say four or six—complete turns forward. By this time, the warp will be tightly twisted; so untwist it by making the same number of complete turns backward (still with one shot of weft at each quarter-turn). This will produce a series of reversed chevrons.

To ensure symmetry, keep tally on a piece of paper of the number of complete turns you make in each direction.

You can try multiple turns on any design that has been set up for the usual 4 quarter-turns forward-and-back procedure.

No Weft

To make a contrast in texture and pattern, try omitting the weft for some distance.

1. Complete a section of pattern, then cut off the weft, and darn the end back into the belt.

2. Move the cards ahead, turning them as you go; the warp forms into a series of four-strand twisted cords.

3. Insert a new weft and weave on in the ordinary way.

4. Further on, after a stretch of ordinary weave, you can repeat the process, turning the cards the opposite way, to unwind the twist in the warp.

5. After moving the cards ahead, you can cross them over each other, rearranging the groups of warp threads so that, when you weave again, you produce a new pattern.

Wrapped Warp

1. Stop weaving at the end of a complete pattern unit, cut off the weft, darn in the end, and move the cards ahead; but for this technique there is no need to turn the cards.

2. Take the warp threads by groups and wrap each group with some yarn of your choice, either matching one of the yarns you are already using, or perhaps something entirely different. (Wrapped warp technique was described in Chapter 4.) You can wrap together the 4 warp threads from each card or the 8 from two cards; you can alternate the size of the groups, 4-8-4-8-4 and so on, right across.

3. With the cards in home position, insert a new weft and begin weaving again.

Braided Band

Use a pattern that can be divided into three symmetrical parts. For example:

	↗	↗ ↘	↘	↗	↗ ↘	↘	↗	↗ ↘	↘			
A	X	O	O	X	X	O	O	X	X	O	O	X
B	X	O	O	X	X	O	O	X	X	O	O	X
C	X	#	#	X	X	#	#	X	X	#	#	X
D	X	#	#	X	X	#	#	X	X	#	#	X
	1	2	3	4	5	6	7	8	9	10	11	12

1. Begin weaving with all 12 cards together. Finish off a pattern unit, then divide the cards into three groups of 4 each. Keep one group in working position; move the other cards forward out of the way, and tie them together with string.

2. Weave with the group of 4 cards; turn them as usual and pass the weft only across the 4 sets of warp threads. Weave a section about 12 inches long, end in home position and tie the 4 cards together.

3. Repeat with the second and third groups of cards, to produce three parallel bands, each ⅓ the total width.

4. Untie the warp at the unwoven end; separate it into three groups, and make a braid of the three narrow bands.

5. Refasten the warp ends and resume weaving right across the band with one weft.

Split Band

Use a pattern with two symmetrical halves. Divide the cards into two groups and, with separate wefts, weave two bands, each half the width of the main band. Then return to weaving all across.

Double Weave

The regular weaving position, with two holes up and two down, makes one shed. But if you put the cards diagonally, with one corner up, you make *two* sheds.

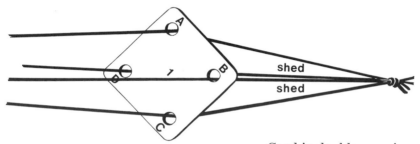

Card in double weaving position.

Warp threads B and D lie close together; there is one shed between A and BD, another between C and BD.

The sheds formed in this diagonal position are narrow; it is easy to misplace the weft, under or over a wrong warp thread. A small flat stick helps to open the correct shed.

Here are three ways to make use of this position.

1. Single Weft. Put the cards in the diagonal position. Pass the weft through the upper shed, and back through the lower shed. Turn the cards a quarter-turn, again to the diagonal position; pass weft again through the upper shed and back through the lower shed. Continue weaving with a quarter-turn between each back-and-forward shot of weft. You make a hollow tube, instead of a flat band of fabric. If you like, before closing off the end of the tube section, you can insert some stuffing, to give this part of the band a thicker, somewhat rounded, contour.

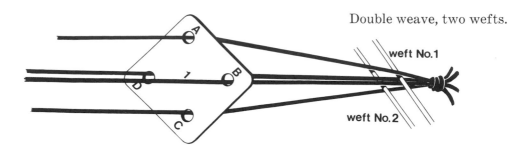

Double weave, two wefts.

2. Two Wefts. Use two separate wefts, one through the upper shed, one through the lower. This makes two separate, parallel bands of the same width. Make a section like this toward the end of a belt, and use it as a means of fastening the belt around your waist; pass the other end through the split section, and pull tight.

You can sew the two bands together down one edge, and make a pocket that will serve as a money-belt.

3. Icelandic Technique. Choose a pattern with two predominant colors evenly distributed, for example, all the A and B holes carry a dark yarn, and all the C and D holes carry a light yarn. Normal weaving produces alternate light and dark bars across the band.

But now put the cards in diagonal position, A uppermost, and pass the weft. (Single-weft or double-weft technique works the same.) Put B uppermost and pass the weft.

Take a quarter-turn back, putting A uppermost, and pass the weft.

Continue like this, first A, then B up. The dark color of A and B will show on one side of the band, the light color of C and D on the other.

Tabby Weave Inserts

To obtain variety of texture—and, if you wish, of color, too—introduce a patch of tabby.

Slide the cards forward, giving them a few turns to twist the warp into a series of 4-stranded cords. Weave a section of the band in tabby, over-one-under-one, treating each 4-strand bundle as a single warp thread. The weft is visible here so, for a color change, you can use a different-colored weft.

CARD WEAVING

Madelaine Chisholm working on a wide, free-form card weaving. Note the cord tied to the bottom bar, so that the weaver can control warp tension with her foot.

Beat in hard, and the weft-color predominates; beat in lightly, leaving the weft threads farther apart, and more of the warp shows through.

Different Home Positions

So far, we have called AD the home position. You can also work from other home positions: AB on top, BC on top, or CD on top. With most threading charts, a change of home position will substantially alter the pattern of the band.

Partial Turns

You can try the effect of 3 quarter-turns forward and 3 back. Also try 5 or 6 quarter-turns forward and back. Each of these will, in most cases, produce a different pattern.

Dyed Warp

If you like to experiment with dyes, you can get unusual, beautiful effects by tie-dyeing or dip-dyeing the warp; the basic pattern will then be repeated, but with different color values at different places along the band.

To create patterns for card weaving, bear in mind these rules.

Lengthwise Stripes. A card threaded in all four holes with yarn of one color makes a stripe of that color all along the band. Two such cards side by side produce a wider stripe, and so on.

Put one or more such cards at each edge, and use weft of that color; then the weft-loops at the selvedges will not be noticeable.

Crosswise Bars. A number of adjoining cards with the same color in the same hole will produce a crosswise bar of that color. If the cards have that color in two adjacent holes, the bar is twice as wide.

Diagonals. A diagonal is made like a crosswise bar, except that the color elements are progressively moved downward instead of going straight across. Here are four cards that could form part of a larger pattern.

A	O	X	X	X
B	X	O	X	X
C	X	X	O	X
D	X	X	X	O

They produce a diagonal of O color on a background of X.

Chevrons and Diamonds. Two diagonals sloping opposite ways make a chevron.

A	O	X	X	X	X	X	X	O
B	X	O	X	X	X	X	O	X
C	X	X	O	X	X	O	X	X
D	X	X	X	O	O	X	X	X

Woven with continuous forward turns, such a pattern produces a series of chevrons. Woven with the ordinary 4 quarter-turns forward and 4 backward, it produces a diamond. (Compare the threading chart on page 139.)

Testing Designs

To test the effect of a design, get some paper ruled in quarter-inch squares; fill in the appropriate squares with the colors carried by each hole of each card. The threading chart thus becomes a colored drawing of the pattern it will produce in 4 quarter-turns.

This advance testing is quicker than buying yarn and starting to weave in order to see what a design looks like.

Other Card Shapes

Three-hole and six-hole cards are sometimes used for card weaving. After you have some experience with the square card, you will find no difficulty in adapting yourself to these other forms.

For bands where great strength is required, a five-hole square card is used. The center hole is threaded with thin string, or a heavy linen thread; this does not show in the pattern, but gives extra strength and resistance to stretching when the band is finished.

FREE-STYLE CARD WEAVING

If you like to produce shapes and patterns spontaneously, you can develop a new, creative approach to card weaving. Warp each card with 4 threads of the same color; then treat the cards as tools for manipulating these warp bundles.

For example: warp 4 cards with brown; 6 with rust; 2 with white; 8 with black, and so on at your discretion, to produce a series of color bands of random widths. This initial color arrangement may be nonsymmetrical or symmetrical, as you choose.

Weave a few inches with the cards in their original order. Now begin to transfer single cards, or groups of cards, from one side to another; turn and twist the design elements; divide and recombine. You might create a design that reminds you of a meandering river, a piece of coral, or other beautiful organic shapes.

There is no need to count the number of turns you make with the cards; simply let your imagination decide when to move a color group in a new direction.

You are not obliged, in this free-style card weaving, to keep the same number of cards throughout. You can add new warp threads —and new cards to carry them—at any time. Here is a technique developed by Byron Johnstad.

To introduce one new card, take 2 warp threads of the chosen color; double them over the last shot of weft, and stretch them out parallel to the original warp. Thread a card on the four ends, and incorporate the card in your weaving from then on.

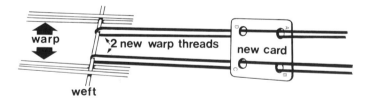

Adding new card.

Mr. Johnstad uses a weaving method that enables him to keep an eye on the whole project as it is developing. He ties the middle of the warp to his belt, and weaves toward himself, beating away from himself. When the completed portion is too close for comfort, he unties the warp and refastens it farther along.

This working position can be used for any kind of card weaving if you find it comfortable.

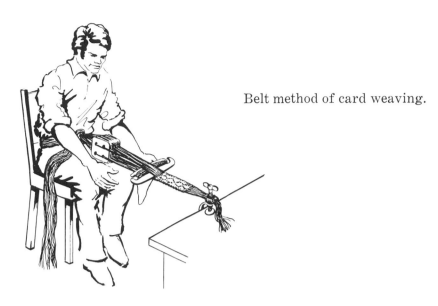

Belt method of card weaving.

However you handle it, this free-style method can be fascinating; you are using the cards as a painter would use his brushes; it is one of the most enjoyable, satisfying techniques available to the creative weaver.

extra lengths of yarn must be knotted onto the end of the web. There are two ways of doing this.

1. Precut Fringe Lengths

a) Cut a number of pieces of yarn a little more than twice the length of the proposed fringe.

b) Fold a piece in half; with a crochet hook, pull the mid-loop through the edge of the finished web.

c) Put the cut ends through the loop to make a Ghiordez knot, and pull tight.

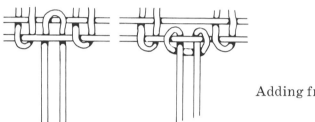

Adding fringe with precut lengths.

For a thicker fringe, pull 2 or 3 pieces of yarn through at once, giving 4 or 6 ends respectively.

2. Uncut Yarn

Instead of precutting the fringe pieces, you can darn in a long piece of yarn with a needle, using a ruler or strip of cardboard to form uniform-sized loops, each held in place by a Ghiordez knot. (This is somewhat like the continuous-weft rug-knotting process described in Chapter 4.)

You may cut the loops, or leave them uncut, as you prefer.

Note

Before a fringe is attached, the end of the web must be made firm, and the weft prevented from unraveling. This should be done while the work is still on the frame. Two methods were described in Chapter 4: finish off with a row of twining; or, finish with a diagonal overcast stitch.

THE PLAIN FRINGE

For some projects, you may like to leave the fringe hanging like this, with no further attempt to ornament it. A plain fringe, provided the yarn is of attractive color and texture, and fairly closely spaced, can look attractive on a carpet, scarf or wall hanging. Nevertheless, many weavers prefer to put in a little extra work on fringes and achieve a more ornamental appearance.

One general rule is worth bearing in mind: a light, delicate web should have a light, delicate fringe structure; a thick, heavy web requires a thick, heavy fringe.

KNOTTED FRINGES

Knotted fringes can vary from extremely simple to extremely complex. Let's begin with the easiest.

Single-Knotted Fringe

Gather the warp ends into groups by twos, threes or fours—even larger numbers if you have a very fine warp—and tie an overhand knot close to the end of the web.

Knotted fringe, 3 warp ends per knot.

Double-Knotted Fringe

1. First make a single-knotted fringe, as described above. For this purpose, each knot must contain 2, 4, 6, or some other even

number of warp ends, because each group is going to be divided in half.

2. For the second row of knots, divide the warp bundles, and tie half of the first to half of the second, with an overhand knot spaced about 1 inch below the first row of knots.

3. Knot the other half of the second bundle to half of the third, and so on.

4. Continue with as many rows of knots as you like.

Double-knotted fringe.

To make an evenly spaced, diamond-shaped array of knots, use a piece of cardboard, or a stick, about 1 inch wide, as a gauge; pass the two groups of warp ends, one each side, and tie the knot flush against the edge.

Note that all the knotted-fringe techniques not only ornament your work; they give extra security against unraveling of the web.

Added Ornaments

You can, if you wish, add extra interest to a knotted fringe by the use of beads. Simply slip a bead of appropriate size and shape over the yarn, or group of yarns, before tying the knot.

TWISTED FRINGE

By this technique, 2 warp ends are twisted together to make one thicker cord, in much the same way as the component parts of a rope are twisted together.

Take 2 warp ends and twist them so as to *tighten* the existing twist of their plies. When they are tightly twisted, hold them together, side by side, and twist them around each other in the opposite direction, so that the two pieces form a 2-stranded yarn, twice as thick. (With some yarns, it may be necessary to repeat the process in order to carry this twisting right down to the ends.)

Twisted fringe.

To prevent the ends from unraveling, tie them in an overhand knot, near the end.

BRAIDED FRINGES

You can take warp ends in groups of 3, 4, or more and braid them into a fringe. Braids look best with firm-textured, smooth-surfaced yarns; they are useless with soft, fluffy yarns.

Three-Strand Braid

This is so well known that no description is necessary.

Five-Strand Braid

This is made on the same general principle as the 3-strand, except that you lay the left-hand yarn over 2 to the right; then

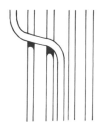 

Five-strand braid.

the right-hand yarn over 2 to the left. Continue like this: left-hand yarn over 2; right-hand yarn over 2, and so on.

Other Odd-Number Braids

Seven, 9, or any odd number of yarns can be braided similarly. For 7, go left-over-3, right-over-3. For 9, go left-over-4, right-over-4.

Four-Strand Braid

Many weavers feel this is the most useful and decorative of the braids.

Lay the right-hand yarn over 1, under 1, *back* over 1 to the right.

Lay the left-hand yarn over 1, under 1, *back* over 1 to the left.

   Four-strand braid.

Repeat this process to form a round braid.

You can get different effects by braiding two pairs of different-colored yarns.

(*a*) Arrange the colored yarns in pairs—for example, red, red, blue, blue—when you start, to produce red and blue stripes running straight down the braid.

(*b*) Arrange the colors alternately—for example, red, blue, red, blue—to produce red and blue spirals.

(*Note*: For best results with this braid, all 4 yarns must be of exactly the same thickness and texture; if one pair is thicker, or stiffer than the other, you will not get the proper symmetrical braid.)

For a thicker braid, use double strands, and make the same braid with the 4 pairs.

Finishing Braids

To prevent unraveling of a braid, tie the ends together with an overhand knot. A more compact finish is to wrap the end of the braid with a single strand of matching yarn. Use the technique illustrated on page 167 to secure the ends of the wrapping yarn without any knots.

Note

Any of these braids may be used, not only for fringes, but to make long, ornamental cords for use as bag handles, etc.

SQUARE-KNOT FRINGE

Take a group of four yarns. Nos. 1 and 4 are the knotting yarns. Nos. 2 and 3 are the stationary warp ends; they simply hang down and form a core around which the knots are tied.

To make the fringe, tie a series of square knots (or reef knots) around the core.

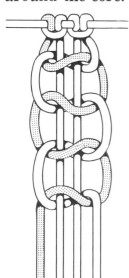

Square-knot fringe.

In the diagram, the knot structure is shown wide open for clarity. In practice, the knots are tightened to lie snugly together. With a thick, fairly soft yarn, the core will be hidden by the knots.

This four-strand "sinnet," as it is called, will hang straight if it is properly made. Some people have a great deal of trouble in producing this effect. The point is that, if yarn No. 1 goes *always over*, or *always under*, the core, the sinnet will be straight.

To make a sinnet with a corkscrew twist, simply tie the knots so that yarn No. 1 goes *alternately over and under* the core.

DOUBLE HALF-HITCH FRINGE

Page 77 showed a method of tying the warp ends in pairs at the bottom of a piece of tapestry. This technique can be adapted to make a fringe. With a piece of matching yarn, tie the warp ends together in groups of 2, 3, 4, or more, using vertical double half-hitches. The knots should be close to the selvedge.

PHILIPPINE FRINGE

This method works best with fairly thick warp yarns. Make a half-hitch with warp end No. 3 around Nos. 1 and 2. Pull it up tight against the web.

With No. 4, make a half-hitch around Nos. 2 and 3. Pull up tight.

Half-hitch No. 5 around Nos. 3 and 4. Pull up tight.

Continue like this right across. In the diagram, the structure is shown loose, for clarity; in practice, the half-hitches are pulled up tight against the end of the web.

Philippine fringe.

TAPESTRY FRINGE

If you have fairly long warp ends, you can use them as the warp for a series of small, tapering tapestry segments in colors and patterns that harmonize with the main web. The last few inches of warp can be finished off by braiding or wrapping, or made into tassels.

TASSELS

Tassels can be made either with warp ends left hanging beyond the end of the web, or by adding new material. Here are some techniques.

1. Wind loops of yarn around your hand, or around a cardboard gauge.

Making tassels: winding the loops; the loops tied and cut.

Hanging cradle, by Dorothy Field. Tapestry with tassels and knotted fringe.

Four examples of tassel and fringe design, by Jo-Anne Ryburn. *No. 1.* Tapestry and wrapped warp. Note the use of two-colored wrappings on the warp ends. *No. 2.* Overhand knots, and wrapped warp holding tufts of feathers. *No. 3.* Overhand knots and ceramic beads. *No. 4.* Groups of warp threads wrapped with fine copper wire, then formed into triple-knotted fringe.

2. Tie a piece of yarn through the top of the loops, fastening them all together; cut the loops at the bottom.

3. Bunch the tied end closely together and wrap yarn tightly around it for about ½ inch. This wrapping may be made with the same yarn as the tassel, or with a contrasting color or material —metallic thread, for example.

Here is the neatest way to secure the wrapping. Begin at the top. Form a narrow loop of the yarn, ½ inch longer than the proposed length of your wrapping, and lay it flat on the tassel, loop end downward.

Securing the wrapping: forming the loop; end of yarn through loop.

Wrap the yarn closely around the tassel, working downward over the two threads of the loop. Then put the loose end of the yarn through the loop.

Now pull on the top end of the yarn till the loop is drawn up *just halfway* inside the wrapping. Cut off the projecting ends.

You can make a wrapping of two or more colors. Suppose you want to work with red and blue. Begin with the red, as described above. After 1 or 2 turns, insert the end of the blue yarn to anchor it.

When you are ready to begin wrapping with the blue, carry the red underneath, and wrap over it with the blue.

Then you can alternate; wrap with red again, and carry the blue under it.

When you have gone far enough, put the last end through the loop and pull up as before.

If necessary, trim the bottom ends of the tassel to hang level. The tie at the top serves to fix it in place.

Tobacco pouch, by Susan Lehman: card weaving and twisted fringe, including bead ornaments.

Detail of card-woven camel pack-strap, from India: cotton and wool. Braided fringes, wrapped warp, and tassels.

Ball Tassel

To make a ball tassel, apply one wrapping as described above. Immediately below this wrapping, insert a bead or marble of appropriate size, and arrange the yarn ends evenly around so that they cover it. Then apply another wrapping close below the ball to hold it in place.

Ball tassel.

A smaller, softer ball tassel can be made without the bead or marble. Make the upper wrapping, then push up some of the tassel yarn to create a bunch or ball immediately below it. Apply the lower wrapping.

POMPONS

A pompon is made on a cardboard form. Suppose you are making a 2-inch pompon.

1. Cut two disks of thin cardboard, 2 inches in diameter; in the center of each disk, cut a hole $3/8$ to $1/2$ inch across.

2. Thread a needle with yarn. Put the two disks one on top of the other, and wrap them together with stitches passing through the center hole and around the edge. To produce a firm, fat pompon, keep these stitches close together; don't skimp on the yarn.

3. When you have stitched all around the disks, take a pair of scissors; slip one blade edgewise between the two disks and cut right around the edge. The cut pieces of yarn spread out to right and left.

4. With a 12-inch piece of matching yarn, tie a tight reef knot around the center of the cut pieces of yarn, between the two cardboard disks. This knot holds the pompon together, and the ends of the yarn will later serve to tie it in place.

5. Remove the cardboard disks. If possible slide them off the cut pieces of yarn; if necessary, cut them off. Fluff up the ends of the pompon into a perfect ball; trim any odd pieces that project and spoil the outline.

Making a pompon: beginning the winding; tying the center.

CHAPTER 13

~~~~~~

BASKET WEAVING

Basket weaving was one of the first crafts developed by primitive man; in most areas it predates pottery and cloth weaving.

The first kind of basketry was wicker weaving, or wattling, the intertwining of sticks and twigs to make huts, pens for livestock, fish weirs and traps.

As people discovered better basket-making materials and techniques, basketry came to serve many purposes: food storage, carrying loads on the backs of men and animals, furniture (stools, chairs, tables, hammocks), clothing (hats, rain capes), beehives, and even boats (the skin-covered coracles of northern Europe).

In some parts of North America, and in Tasmania, the craft developed to the point where baskets were woven so finely as to be watertight! They were even used for cooking, by dropping hot stones into the water until it boiled.

Different materials were used in different parts of the world—

grass, straw, flax, cane, and bamboo. Colors were produced by dyeing the materials, decorations by incorporating beads, feathers and other ornaments. In some regions, each family or town had its traditional, exclusive designs.

Pottery developed from basketry. A basket lined with clay was accidentally left too near the fire; the basket burned off, and there was left the first pot, a hard-fired vessel with basket marks on its surface. So, for a long time, people used baskets as molds for their pottery; from the imprints on these pots we can learn the weaving patterns used by prehistoric peoples.

No machine has yet been invented that will satisfactorily weave baskets; it is still a handcraft, and many of the techniques have remained substantially unchanged for centuries, and are practiced in many different parts of the world.

The purpose of this chapter is to acquaint you with three basic methods of basketry; with this knowledge, you will be able to produce, not only conventionally shaped baskets, but exciting new forms—baskets specially designed for your own needs, hats, masks, wall plaques, sculptures.

The three methods, in brief, are: *plaiting*, in which warp and weft are interwoven diagonally; *coiling*, in which the warp is wrapped with the weft, and formed into coils, which are sewn together; *weaving*, in which the warp consists of a number of rigid elements called spokes, and the weft is a softer, more pliable material, such as raffia or fine rattan cane.

MATERIALS

Materials commonly used for the warp structure are cane, grasses, rushes, twigs, pine needles, split bamboo, birch bark, cedar bark, rope, string, and wire.

Raffia, Swiss straw (a synthetic material much like cellophane), string, wool, sisal, jute, and feathers are used for weaving and wrapping.

Some of these materials need a little preparation before use.

Cane

Basket cane is made from the center portion of the stem of the rattan palm, a tropical climbing plant. (The shiny outer part, cut into strips, is used for making cane chairs.) It comes in a range of thicknesses, from about $\frac{1}{16}$ inch up to about $\frac{1}{4}$ inch; you would normally select a thickness proportional to the size of the basket you are making.

When dry, the cane is hard and springy, and in this state it would be very difficult to work with. So, before use, soak the cane for 10 minutes in warm water; this makes it soft and pliable. As it dries out, after being woven, it gets hard again, so the basket retains its shape. If a piece of cane begins to dry too soon, and becomes hard to handle, moisten it again with a damp sponge or cloth.

Rushes

Rushes are widely available for the picking in swamps. After gathering, they must be *thoroughly* dried, or they will rot. (The same applies to grass, reeds, or any other plant products.) This drying removes the sap, but it leaves the rushes very brittle; if you tried to weave them in this state, they would crumble to pieces.

So prepare the rushes a day ahead of time. Soak them in water for an hour, and let them lie under a wet towel overnight; they will be soft and flexible when you weave, but will become stiff again as the finished basket dries out.

Willow

Thin, young willow twigs are excellent for basketry. They can be used with the bark on, or peeled. They peel quite easily while fresh and green. You can hold the end of the twig in your teeth (if they are strong enough!) and strip off the bark with your fingernails.

As with cane and rushes, willow twigs should first be dried, then moistened again before you begin to work with them.

Raffia

You can dye raffia to a wide range of colors with Ciba dyes.

String

If string is dipped in melted beeswax, it will work more easily, and the finished basket will have a nice shine.

Sisal

Sisal tends to be rather stiff; dampen it a bit, and it becomes more pliable.

Feathers

Wet feathers before use; then you can bend and twist the quill, and wrap over the quill to attach it firmly.

EQUIPMENT

A bodkin or a curved sailmaker's needle is needed for the coiled technique.

An old glove, or a sailmaker's "palm," is useful. It prevents your hand from getting sore when pushing needles through the basket coils, and when pulling the wrapping yarn tight.

For cutting cane, you need a sharp knife or a pair of pruning shears.

Mrs. Victor Massajesva weaving a basket. Note that the cane spokes are used in groups of three. (*Photo: Ulli Steltzer*)

THE PLAITED BASKET

In this method, begin by making a long braid of some suitable material such as rushes. Make three bundles of the rushes, each about ¾ inch in diameter; tie them to a hook in the wall, and plait them into a 3-strand braid. Keep adding rushes to lengthen the bundles and to maintain them at the same thickness.

When you have enough of the braid, coil it to form the basket shape you desire; sew the coils together about every half-inch with 3-ply string.

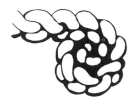

Coiling the braid.

For the bottom of a big basket, put the braid on edge vertically, and sew the coils together, side to side; this gives a thick, strong bottom to the basket. For the sides, keep the braids vertical and sew them together edge to edge.

For a small basket, it will be adequate to lay the braids flat on the bottom and sew them edge to edge.

Because the braids are quickly made, and are so thick, this is a very fast method of making baskets; but if it is carefully done, the resulting basket looks neat and attractive, and will be quite strong.

THE COILED BASKET

The coiled basket technique corresponds somewhat to the wrapped warp. (Or, if you have ever made a coiled pot, you will discover the similarity between these pottery and basketry techniques.) You take a long piece of cane, rope, twisted grass, or some similar material; wrap around it another flexible material—string, wool, raffia, for example—and twist it into a spiral coil. After every one or more turns of wrapping, the newly formed coil is fastened to the previous coil by overcasting. If done with care, this technique produces baskets of great structural strength.

Here is an important point: the softer the core of your coil, the easier it is to work with. Wool roving, for example, is light; you can use one strand, or ply several strands together, and the bodkin will easily go through. A stiffer material, such as a heavy rope, will produce a strong basket form that might serve very well for a sculpture, but not for a shopping basket.

(Cane is difficult to use for this technique; I would advise you not to try it until you have had some practice with easier materials.)

1. Take a piece of soft rope, about the thickness of clothesline. (Alternatively, you can use twisted grass, or some similar material, of the same thickness.) Cut the end of the rope to a point. Thread a bodkin with 3 or 4 feet of raffia, and begin wrapping the rope tightly with raffia about 1 inch from the end; wind the raffia around the rope, to the pointed end, and back again. Then continue wrapping along the rope.

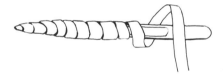

Wrapping the end of the rope.

2. After you have wrapped a few inches, bend the point into a spiral and hold it in place with a figure-8 stitch to the next turn. This first coil should be tightly made, with only a tiny hole in the center.

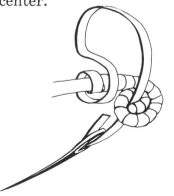

The first spiral.

3. Now continue wrapping. The procedure is: twice around the rope; overcast to the next turn; twice around; overcast again, and so on. Take care to pull the raffia very tight on every turn and overcast; this ensures a firm structure for the basket.

Three completed turns and overcast.

4. Adding new raffia. When you get nearly to the end of a piece of raffia, drive the needle right through the rope; cut off the end so as to leave 1 inch protruding. Thread a new length of 3 or 4 feet through the needle, drive this right through the rope, and continue winding. Bind the ends of the old and new pieces tightly to the rope, laying them in the grooves so as not to form a bulge.

5. Making the sides. When you have made a circular shape about 6 inches in diameter, start forming the sides. Lay the next coil on top of the previous one. By laying up the side coils vertically, you will make a cylindrical shape; if you make each coil a little wider than the one below it, you will have an outward-slanting shape.

6. Finishing off. When the sides are high enough, taper the end of the core, and wrap and overcast it to the previous coil.

Variations

Here are some alternate techniques you can use to produce different textures, shapes, and color effects in your coiled baskets.

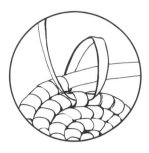

Two-turns-and-stitch method.

1. *Stitching.* Wrap 2 turns around the core as usual; but then, instead of overcasting right around the previous coil, just take a stitch through the wrapping material of the previous coil.

Split-core method.

2. *Split core.* Divide the core into halves; wrap only one of the halves, and leave the other exposed. This, of course, will be most successful with a core material that is visually interesting, such as pine needles, unspun sisal, etc.

3. *Core loops.* Instead of simply laying the core around and around in uniform coils, you can use it to form loops or other sculptural forms.

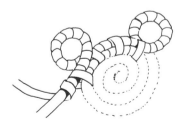

Core loops.

4. *Multicolored wrapping.* You can use your wrapping material to create color designs on the basket. Suppose, for example, you choose green, blue, and beige. Lay the green and blue threads along the core and wrap with the beige. To change color, use the

blue as the working thread, covering up the green and beige. Then wrap with the green and cover up the blue and beige.

If you wish to plan a symmetrical pattern, find the exact distance around your basket; see how many turns of wrapping material are needed to cover 1 inch of core; then draw your design on graph paper.

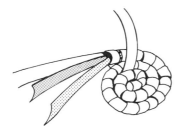 Multicolored wrapping.

Rush Base

Dried rushes make a good core material for coiled baskets. Form them in bundles ½ to ¾ inch in diameter and wrap firmly with raffia, or some other yarn of your choice. Keep adding fresh rushes as you go, to maintain the bundle at an even thickness and to make it as long as is necessary for your project.

Pine Needles

Long pine needles can similarly be formed into a base for making coils; keep adding new needles as you wrap. Form the basket just as you would with coiled rope or string. (These needles will emit a pleasant aroma for a long time.)

Cane Base

After some practice with softer materials, you may like to try using cane. Wool makes a good wrapping material with cane; be-

Coiled basket and placemats, by Audrey Williams: raffia with pine needles as filler.

cause it is soft, it spreads a little as you wind it, and covers the ground more quickly than would a harder yarn like sisal. (If you do use sisal, wet it; it works better wet than dry.) Natural raffia and the synthetic raffias are also good with cane; so are some of the tough, colored strings sold for parcel-tying.

THE WOVEN BASKET

The woven basket, like a piece of cloth, has a warp and weft. A number of strong, stiff canes or wires radiate from the center of the base, like the spokes of a wheel, and stand up more or less vertically in the sides of the basket. On them is woven the weft (sometimes called the weaver), a thinner, more flexible material such as rattan, raffia, string, or jute.

The Base

1. Take 8 canes. Lay them in a cross formation, four-over-four.

2. Take a thin rattan and fold it in two (though not exactly in half: it's easier to join on new lengths of rattan later if the two parts don't end at the same spot). Form a tight loop around the first arm of the cross; twist alternately around the other three arms. Similarly weave right around once more.

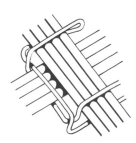

The cane cross.

In this diagram, the double rattan is shown loose, for clarity. In practice, it should be tightly pulled in against the arms of the cross.

3. Now spread out the 8 canes like the spokes of a wheel. Continue weaving around and around, going over and under each cane in turn with the two ends of the rattan.

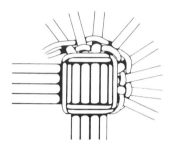

The base canes spread out.

(*Note.* If the base canes are rather stiff, you will find it easier first to spread them out into four pairs, and weave two complete turns, over-two-and-under-two, before proceeding to weave over-one-and-under-one.)

4. To join on new lengths of rattan smoothly, splice the ends; cut both ends on a diagonal so they overlap and the join comes on top of one of the spokes.

5. Continue weaving around and around till you have a circular base about 6 inches across.

The Sides

When you are ready to form the sides, bend the spokes up at right angles. (If the cane has dried out, it may need to be wetted again at the bend.) Tie the top ends of the spokes loosely together with string; this prevents them from springing back to the old position.

African coiled and beaded baskets. Geometric patterns produced by using
two colors of wrapping.

Now continue weaving around the sides, one weft end under and one over each spoke—just the same weave as you used on the base. Splices in the rattan should now come on the inner side of a spoke. (Closely study a commercially made basket if you have trouble with this.)

When the sides are high enough, stop weaving. Cut off the spokes 2 inches above the top of the weaving, and bend the ends back into the weave.

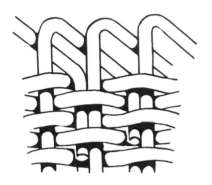

Finishing off the rim.

Trim the weft ends neatly so that they lie just inside the rim.

Variations

After you have mastered the basic technique, you can begin to treat the warp more creatively.

When you have made a secure base, you can divide the spokes into small groups, weaving each group separately for a while, then joining them together again. You can bend one group of spokes out, treating them as a separate unit, and then work them in again. Use the wrapped-warp technique on single spokes or small groups. Cross the spokes; bend them; twist them.

With these ideas, you will be able to create lovely, sculptural effects with your basketry.

Coiled basketry wall plaque, by Elizabeth Alexander, of Long Island State
College: multicolored jute and wool wrapping on sisal filler.

Coiled basket, by Audrey Williams: multicolored sisal wrapping on heavy rope filler. Note how the filler is used to make the handle.

Four baskets by students of Long Beach State College. *Left to right,* waxed linen wrapping on sisal filler, with seashells; by Debra Kotoff. Miniature basket; sewing-thread wrapping on cane filler; by Linda Lewis. Woven basket with wrapped segments; reed, linen, and wool; by Judy Wilson. Waxed linen and feathers on jute filler; by Robert Granados.

Coiled basket, by Robert Granados of Long Beach State College: cotton wrapping with feathers on jute filler.

SUPPLIERS OF WEAVING MATERIALS AND EQUIPMENT

U.S.A.

Contessa Yarns, 3-5 Bailey Avenue, Ridgefield, Connecticut 06877, U.S.A.

Folklorico, P.O. Box 625, 442 Ramona St., Palo Alto, California 94302, U.S.A.

Lily Mills Company, Shelby, North Carolina 28150, U.S.A.

Robin & Russ Handweavers, 533 North Adams St., McMinnville, Oregon 97128, U.S.A.

Shuttlecraft, P.O. Box 6041, Providence, Rhode Island 02904, U.S.A.

Troy Yarn and Textile Company, 603 Mineral Springs, Pawtucket, Rhode Island 02862, U.S.A.

The Yarn Depot, 545 Sutter Street, San Francisco, California 94102, U.S.A.

CANADA

Briggs & Little Woolen Mills Ltd., York Mills, York County, New Brunswick, Canada

William Condon & Sons, Box 129, Charlottetown, P.E.I., Canada

Curl Bros. Specialties, 334 Lauder Avenue, Toronto 10, Ontario, Canada

Handcraft House, 110 West Esplanade, North Vancouver, British Columbia, Canada

Handcraft Wools, Box 378, Streetsville, Ontario, Canada

Mrs. T. Palvio (Finnish linen and wool), Chelsea, Quebec, Canada

NEW ZEALAND

Cambridge Wools Ltd., 16-22 Anzac Ave., P.O. Box 2572, Auckland, New Zealand

NORWAY

Norsk Kunstvergarn A/S, 4892 Homborsund, Grimstad 4317, Norway

SWEDEN

Borgs of Lund, P.O. Box 1096, S-22104, Lund 1, Sweden

DENMARK

Cum Textile Industries Ltd., 5 Roemersgade, 1362 Copenhagen, Denmark

GERMANY

Friedrich Traub, Waiblingen (Wuertt), Post O. Box 65, Germany

UNITED KINGDOM

The Multiple Fabric Co., Ltd., Dudley Hill, Bradford 4, England